NO

NETWORK MARKETING
THE IVY LEAGUE WAY

DEGREE
REQUIRED

AMY POWERS

HARVARD LAW SCHOOL, JD
COLUMBIA BUSINESS SCHOOL, MBA

Published by Winsome Entertainment Group LLC

Library of Congress Cataloging-in-Publication Data

Powers, Amy.
No Degree Required: Network Marketing the Ivy League Way
ISBN: 978-5136-7542-8

This book is dedicated to the memory of

my beloved father, Marty Powers,

whose entrepreneurial spirit,

fearless journey of reinvention,

and unwavering support

of my dreams inspire me daily.

Table of Contents

Introduction: I'm an Ivy League Network Marketer

    (And You Can Be One, Too)   1

Chapter 1: It's Crazy – or IS It?   7

Chapter 2: My Story (Everyone's Got One)   13

Chapter 3: Network Marketing: What It Is   22

Chapter 4: Network Marketing: What It Isn't   39

Chapter 5: A Smart Business for Smart People   46

Chapter 6: Yeah, But   56

Chapter 7: Find Your Fit   71

Chapter 8: Use the Blueprint to Build   84

Chapter 9: If at First You Don't Succeed   102

Chapter 10: People, Purpose, and Passion Are Required,

    Not Optional   112

Chapter 11: More Ivy League Tips to the Top   126

Resource List   147

Introduction

I'm an Ivy League Network Marketer (And You Can Be One, Too)

Many people are curious about why an Ivy Leaguer – a Vassar College, Columbia Business School and Harvard Law School graduate – would embrace Network Marketing, a profession a lot of people still regard with suspicion. And why, after ten years in the profession, I still bound out of bed, totally pumped to offer Network Marketing to the world.

First, as a professional Network Marketer, I'm earning more money than I did as a real estate finance lawyer in a major NY firm (my first career), and I'm earning money more consistently than I did when I was solely a songwriter (my second career). I love what I do now, and I did it without leaving the past behind – just the parts I didn't like.

Next, I am itching... no, actually, *burning*... to change some misconceptions about the Network Marketing profession. For every forward-thinking person I know who is *all about* Network Marketing, or Social Marketing as it's often now called, there's another who has a judgment about it. I experience this on a regular basis. If I introduce myself as a Harvard-trained lawyer with an MBA from Columbia University, I often get what I call "the Approving Nod" (as in, "Now *you*, Amy, have done well for yourself.") But if I introduce myself as a professional Network Marketer, I get the raised eyebrow, the blank stare or what I call "the Sneer" ("Poor gal. Must have hit hard times. Imagine having to do one of *those* things.") Which to my mind is just plain nuts! My life is ten times **better** since I started my Network Marketing business!

I actually have an amazing life. I wake up when I want to, I work when I want to, I do yoga when I want to. I hang out with whomever I want, whenever I want. I chill with my kids and my husband… a LOT. I help charities that I'm passionate about. I have delightful, inspiring colleagues and teammates. I feel totally supported by and connected to my work community. And I'm HAPPY when I check my bank statements.

It's crazy to me that there are so many otherwise intelligent, open-minded people who are still suspicious of, or even sledgehammer judgmental about, what I do. And that they are ready to bring that hammer DOWN! Why? Are they misinformed or just uninformed? I earn more now than I did before. I'm joyful now when I was miserable before. I am helping more people now than I ever did before. And perhaps most importantly, I can show anyone how to have what I have now, and I couldn't before. So… HUH?

Look, no one wants to be duped, or had, or taken for a ride. We're all a little self-protective. Maybe even leery. If this is you… I totally get it. Because I WAS you. But – maybe like you – I was experiencing a few things that weren't working 100% in my life. I didn't know – until a stranger introduced *me* to this business model – that Network Marketing might be the brilliant solution that was hiding in plain sight. And even after I was introduced, I didn't truly believe it was real, or if it was, that it could ever be a fit for me personally.

But it *was* real. And it *was* a fit. It took me a minute – ok, multiple minutes – but I went from arms-crossed naysayer to enlightened evangelist. Why? The reasons are many, but first and foremost, it was because Network Marketing is actually genius! In my second decade as a professional Network Marketer, I am more committed than ever to sharing this business model, and its value in today's world, with as many people as I can.

And just to be transparent: **I'm not here to convince you of anything**. Network Marketing professionals are not in the convincing business. We're in the sorting business, in the recommending business, and the businesses of teaching, coaching, igniting, and inspiring. And, oh yeah – in the sales business.

I do want to educate you, though. If my Ivy League years taught me one thing, it's that education is key. So, I'll teach you everything I've learned. If you end up deciding to have your own Network Marketing business, I don't want you to be just any old Network Marketer. Lord knows the world has plenty of those. I want you to be an **Ivy League Network Marketer**.

What do I mean by that?

According to Merriam-Webster Dictionary, the Ivy League is "a group of long-established eastern U.S. colleges and universities widely regarded as high in scholastic and social prestige." Harvard, Columbia, Yale, Princeton, Dartmouth, Brown, Cornell, and the University of Pennsylvania, to be precise.

According to the Urban Dictionary, the Ivy League is "the place your parents wanted you to go, but even your dumb ass knew you wouldn't get in!"

Choose whatever definition you like better. To me, "Ivy League" is simply a shorthand for top-notch. Gold standard. Steeped in tradition, yet leading in innovation. Somewhere you can always find smart, ambitious people who go above and beyond, continually striving for excellence.

In this book, I'll show you the Ivy League way to *think* about Network Marketing, and the Ivy League way to *do* Network Marketing. I'll give you a top-notch diagnostic to help you determine whether the business model might be for you. I'll explain what Network Marketing is and isn't in today's economy, and how it's steeped in tradition, yet leading in innovation. I'll clarify the Network Marketing edge in our changing technological and consumer landscapes. I'll explain why it attracts smart, ambitious people who are rewarded for learning to go above and beyond. I'll share stories from inspiring, everyday folks – in my own company and others – who've created satisfying, meaning-filled lives via successful Network Marketing businesses. Then you can make an educated choice about whether it's for YOU.

If you decide to say yes to Network Marketing, I'll show you how to find the right company to work with, then walk you through the gold standard Blueprint of what to do first, next, and after that to have as much success with your business as you desire. I'll reveal my own "bush league to Ivy League" Network Marketing journey so you can see that doubt isn't a death sentence. I'll instruct you on how to strive for excellence by avoiding the twin time sucks of fear and frustration, and their dreaded corollary, **earnorexia**! And to help you bring power to your pursuit, I'll share my Ivy League Tips to the Top, which will help you anticipate and resolve common Network Marketing challenges.

If you're already a fan of the Network Marketing model, congrats! I hope to help you strengthen your conviction and expand your knowledge.

If you're a total Network Marketing skeptic, fantastic! I hope to help you feel comfortably curious about deciding if Network Marketing is a fit for you.

If it turns out to be for you, great!

If it turns out not to be for you, that's totally fine. However, you likely know someone who might benefit in a life-changing way from knowing about this profession. If so, **I highly recommend** that you share this information with them.

And if someone you love – or even just like – has given you this book because you seem utterly disapproving of their professional Network Marketing aspirations, excellent. Take a read through anyway. It just might help you decide to buy their products. It might spur you on to introduce them to some people who you think will enjoy these products, or their business, too. It could lead you to admire their courage. Or inspire you to cheer for their successes. And maybe… just maybe… it might even open your mind about the value of this type of biz for yourself.

If you choose to join this profession, you'll be equipped to approach your Network Marketing business the Ivy League Way – whether you already have a wall full of diplomas or you never went to college at all. I mean, if an Ivy Leaguer is smart enough to do this, you can be too… tuition-free. So, let's get to campus, shall we?

Chapter 1

It's Crazy – or IS It?

Are you truly happy right now? I sincerely hope so. But if you're not, it's not surprising. And it's not necessarily your fault. Life is ever more unpredictable, juggling everyday demands ever trickier, and satisfaction ever more elusive. There are SO many people who are silently – or screamingly – discontent with the trajectory of their lives, who don't know that Network Marketing offers a potential answer as close as their Smartphone.

Before we dive into the details of the business model, you'll need to decide whether there's even a chance you'd be a candidate for this kind of thing. Ask yourself: Are you open? Warm? Honest? Coachable? Do you like helping people? If you answered yes for each, great. Those are all prerequisites to becoming an Ivy League Network Marketer.

Next, diagnose yourself. Do you have one or more of these top 10 common modern era symptoms that signify Network Marketing MIGHT be for you? You can call it your Ivy League entrance exam – except no one is going to grade you but you.

1. Your Day Job is a Nightmare.

It happens. And it's ok to admit. But let's clarify: are you sick OF your job... or sick FROM your job? If you are sick OF your job, you are not alone. You're in the majority. According to a

Gallup Poll of the American Workplace, of the country's approximately 100 million full-time employees, 67% either feel no connection to their jobs, or actually resent them. Worldwide, that statistic is 85%.

If you're sick FROM your job, I feel you. Being a lawyer made me literally ill with chronic fatigue syndrome. Law was a great fit for my bank account, but a lousy fit for my body, not to mention my soul. Nothing against the legal profession – it's awesome for the right type of person. I just wasn't her. So, if you are sick FROM your job, your body could be telling you that something needs to change.

2. Your Work Just Isn't Working for You.

You don't have to be sick of your job or sick from your job to be feeling like something's off. Maybe the economics of your industry are shifting in a way that makes you uneasy. Maybe you've outgrown your cubicle. Maybe at 27 you trained to be a dental hygienist and it was great, but now you're 47, and you don't want to put your fingers into anyone else's mouth but your own. Maybe you simply feel you're not growing. Or your energy's not flowing. Maybe you just get the feeling you were made for more.

And of course, you don't need an actual "job" to feel this way. You can be "working" as a stay-at-home mom, as a volunteer organizer, as a solopreneur, an entrepreneur, an unpaid intern…and it can be working for you, or not.

3. You are Currently Job-Free.

If you don't have a job and it's because you have a big fat trust fund (my family calls this "Lucky Sperm Club") or you have a big fat lust fund (what we call it when your life is paid for by someone who thinks you're hot), congrats! Network Marketing may not be your jam. (Though it still might be, because you might see it as a vehicle for social change, community, or philanthropy.)

But if the reason you don't have a job is because you've been sidelined from the workforce by illness or injury – your own or that of someone you love – or just by a topsy turvy economy, you might be in the right place because this is one profession where you can never be "hired" or "fired."

4. You've Got Student Loan Debt – Whether You're a Student or a Parent.

Awkward congrats – you're part of a huge club of which no one enjoys being a member. In the U.S. alone, you're one of 44.7 million people who have traded learning for loans, averaging almost $33,000 per student. Or you're one of the 3.6 million generous Parent PLUS loan borrowers who borrowed money to help pay a child's educational costs. Your average loan is $25,600.

You might be fresh out of college, or someone who went to school decades ago and still has unpaid debt. Or maybe you're one of the 25% of private student loan cosigners ages 50 and older who had to make a loan payment because your student borrower failed to do so. If you're younger, just having loan payments can feel like a burden. And the older you get, the more the financial strain likely comes at an inopportune moment in your earnings timeline. Blech.

5. **You've Gone to an Institution of Higher Learning but You're not Higher Earning.**

If you're a recent grad, you're one of over 40% who doesn't have a full-time job six months after graduation. At two years after college, you're part of the 43.5% who feel you're underemployed. You either have a full-time job, but believe it doesn't put your education, experience, or training to work, or you're working part-time when you'd rather have a full-time job. Later on, your odds of having a job go up to approximately 90%, but you still might feel that you're not getting paid what you're worth.

6. **You're Tired of Betting on a Broken Employment System.**

The old-school model of getting a degree, working for 40 years at 40 hours a week, and retiring comfortably with a pension is gone, never to return. Whereas companies used to be places you could count on for the long haul, now the average time at any job you get in the U.S. is 4 years. Not to mention outsourcing, downsizing, pandemic-related disruptions, and the benefits-free joy of the Gig Economy (or as I call it, the Gag Economy). You might be ready to bet on yourself in a new way.

7. **You're Earning a Lot but Don't Have the Time or Energy to Enjoy Your Money.**

You're in the happy minority of highly-paid people; however for you, earning and fulfillment aren't going hand in hand. You might be feeling "time-poor" because there just aren't enough hours in the day to practice your profession, plus engage in hobbies, philanthropy, or meaningful time with family or friends. Or maybe your work takes so much physical or emotional effort that it's wearing you down. Whichever the case, you can't take advantage of the other things the world has to offer and might want to explore a way to ultimately have more balance.

8. **You're at a Crossroads.**

You've made some choices, and they've led you to where you are, but you still feel like you're missing a map to the next destination. You're ready for the next chapter, if only you knew what that looked like. You're stuck at a decision point. You're past the past, but you can't see the future. And you can go this way, or go that way, but you can't just keep standing there forever.

9. **You'd Rather Potentially Get Paid than Just Pay.**

Like it or not, we buy stuff all the time. Imagine if just some of that stuff cost less, and could even make you money. You've gotten hip to the fact that, while most people are simply *paying* for their stuff, some people have created businesses where they can potentially *get paid* because of the stuff they choose to use. You'd rather be like them.

10. You are Silently Suffering.

You aren't necessarily broadcasting it, but the truth is that you are dealing with financial stress, or ageism, sexism, racism, a less than abundant life, a less than exciting life, a less than connected life, a less than balanced life... **and have been secretly hoping, yearning, perhaps even praying for a change.**

If any of the above rings a bell, Network Marketing MIGHT be the opportunity to join me to achieve everything I've received from my Network Marketing business: money, purpose, peace of mind, freedom, challenge, triumph, community, support, mad personal growth, and the ability to offer anyone who wants the same to have the chance to get it for themselves.

If that bell is ringing, I feel you. I'll share my story to show you there is no shame or blame in putting down checkmarks next to these issues. Believe me, I had at least half of these covered.

Chapter 2

My Story (Everyone's Got One)

I definitely do not want to give you the impression that my life has always been sunshine and roses, that I grew up with a silver spoon, or simply started Network Marketing on a lark. Um, nah. While my life's full of fun, freedom, purpose, and passion NOW, it wasn't always.

Let's turn back the clock:

Thirty years ago. Monday, 6 a.m. Manhattan. Alarm clock rings. Ugh. I stumble out of bed. The quickest shower, and then I put on this sexless straightjacket 'dress for success' suit. Steel myself against the New York winter cold, zone out on the subway, fight the crowds, make it up to the 37th floor of a monolithic tower, past corridors of cubicles, to my shared cell... I mean office. Dull dull dull. Why didn't anyone warn me?

I know that this is one of the best law firms in the world. That hundreds of hungry graduates apply for every position and that I should feel LUCKY to have this job. But all that registers is how numb I am. I am the smallest cog in the biggest wheel. My soul is shrinking, my brain is atrophying, and I'm not even 30. I spent ALL these years in school for THIS? Why does everyone else appear perfectly happy when I am SO miserable?

I have lunch delivered to the conference room, and by the time I'm done with endless case documents, it's dark again. It's been twelve billable, but joyless, hours.

I don't care how much it pays, this 'dream job' is anything but a dream.

Twenty years ago. Monday, 6 a.m. Venice Beach. I wake up with a song in my head, as usual. And I am going to record that song right away. Ya-freakin'-hoo! I've escaped. Songwriting is MUCH more 'me' than the whole corporate Wall Street lawyer thing. And MUCH better! Except when it's not. Which is… well, kinda always. Because freelance is not for sissies. You can never predict when the money's coming. And everyone is fishing in the same pretty small pond – there are only so many artists, and so many albums a year.

But I'm ok, because I LOVE being a creative. Except when my car payment is due. Or when I want some new clothes. Or would like to get moving on that retirement account. I mean, I'm not a kid anymore. And in fact, I've met this great guy, Todd, and we're thinking about getting married… and he's a freelancer too. Hmmm.

Ten years ago. Monday, 6 a.m. Los Angeles: A bolt of fear, cold and ruthless, wakes me up. It's like this every morning now.

I don't know what's scarier – the fact that the money is suddenly going out faster than it's coming in, the fact that I'm completely unsure what to do about that, or the fact that I'm so exhausted – again – that I literally can't get out of bed. Which is a big problem, because I need to get the kids some breakfast and Todd is already at work. Some days my hands feel so heavy that I can't even lift them. Other days I need to sleep from noon to 3 just to muddle through until nightfall.

Everything feels out of control. There's a *massive* worldwide recession. Plus, songs have become free to download – so *my entire industry is going off the rails.* Whoever said, "Do what you love and the money will follow" wasn't in the music biz right now.

But I don't want to stop writing. Writing is my calling. I just want to stop having to worry about the money, the mortgage, the whole shebang.

I can't bear to go back to being a lawyer... no matter how much it would pay. And I definitely don't want to go back to school – how much more would that cost, and what kind of assurance would I have that I'd a) get hired, b) find something that would let us thrive, c) allow me to take a 3-hour nap on any given afternoon?

What's a smart girl like me doing in a stupid situation like this? I'm 48 years old, with two young kids and no Plan B. I'm sick, I'm stuck, and I'm SCARED.

Are you following me? Can you relate? How's your health? Your self-esteem? Your enthusiasm for your current situation? Are you chasing a big dream with a butterfly net? Or have you put all your dreams on a shelf in the back of the closet? Be honest. Take a minute, close this book and get real with yourself.

In my case, NO ONE knew I was dying a little more inside every day. At least I hope not, because I spent a ton of effort trying not to show it. The boys were healthy, we had a lovely home, lots of friends, and we were always busy. If anyone asked me, or looked at my social media, everything was fine, fine, totally fine. In other words, I had my LA face on. But please.

The crazy thing is that I thought it was just me – the work not working, my feeling sick and stressed. I blamed myself. I shamed myself… which only made it worse. And I knew I needed a solution. I just had no idea what it was.

Then out of the blue, one winter morning, everything changed.

I opened my email to find a note from my Emmy-winning collaborator Michèle – one of the most business savvy songwriter-producers in my world. It read, "Hi Amy – a really successful music publisher I know has started a new business. She's looking for entrepreneurial partners and I thought of you. Are you interested?"

Um, DUH. Yes!

And that's how I was introduced to Linda Blum Huntington, who became my personal Network Marketing mentor and dear friend. But not right away. First, I put her, her company, and her whole business model through the wringer.

Linda and I had an instant rapport. She was brilliant and hilarious, all fun and no BS. I was excited to hear what kind of clever new music business she had that, I imagined, could magically bring my family and me back to living life in style. So I was gobsmacked when she told me that her new venture had nothing to do with music.

Linda explained that she had started a business with a major health, wellness, and beauty brand that offered a one-stop shop for clean, high performance, vegan versions of everyday products. Things we all use, run out of, and go back and buy again: skin care, hair care, body products, make-up, nutrition. What the business world calls Daily Consumable Products. And this brand offered Daily Consumable Products from head to toe, inside and out, at every age and stage of life.

Well, I reasoned, *that's pretty genius. I mean, if you're going to pick a new business, pick one that offers things everyone uses all the time, and will never stop using.*

She told me that she was showing people how to simply redirect the money they were already spending on products to this safe brand. At a great discount if they wanted.

Cool. Because I am allergic to paying full price for anything.

And that anyone who became an Independent Consultant with the company could not only do that, but have the opportunity to earn money as well.

Ooh, money! Tell me more! I wash, eat, and drink anyway... if I can find a way to get paid, so much the better!

And the whole thing was online.

Sweet! So instead of the internet being my royalty-killing enemy, it could be my financial friend. I mean, you can't download shampoo.

Plus, it was designed to be part-time, and the company's compensation plan was truly generous.

WOW. I was INTO this.

Then Linda asked me two questions that rocked me back on my heels.

First: "If you keep doing *exactly* what you're doing right now, where will you be in five years...especially financially... and how will that FEEL?"

Second: "If something happened to your family's main source of income, how long could you comfortably rely on your savings?"

Yikes, right?

Then she paused and said, "So, Amy... do you want to jump in and do this with me?"

I wish I could tell you that I screamed hallelujah and signed up on the spot. What I actually said was, "I HAVE TO THINK ABOUT IT."

And I completely understand you may feel the same way too. Why? Because even though half of me was shouting, "Let's go!" the other half was screaming, "Not so fast." I am a lawyer and an MBA for crying out loud – in other words, a trained skeptic.

I immediately began to internally argue my case for why this business couldn't or shouldn't be my answer. *If this company is so great, why haven't I heard of it before? And why isn't this brand offered in stores – is it not good enough? Do these products even actually work? Are businesses like this actually even LEGIT?*

And on top of the professional case I'm building to counter what Linda is saying, I heap a pile of personal roadblocks:

A beauty brand? Me? That's a joke… I'm lucky if I wash my face.

Nutrition is NOT my mission. I mean, my idea of dinner is the kids' leftover Trader Joe's pizza crusts, a very large glass of Chardonnay, and a hunk of dark chocolate. OK, the whole bar.

And wouldn't I have to be a "pushy salesperson?" Yuck.

Plus, let's be realistic, I'm already exhausted. I don't have one more minute for one more thing on my plate.

You can see why I didn't say "yes" from the get-go, and why I understand you may not be willing to either. But … I didn't say no. Because I was still curious. Because it was intuitively sensible. Because I hated my answers to those two questions Linda asked. And because I needed my solution.

For **four months,** I went full detective on the whole Network Marketing thing. I started from scratch, because this type of business wasn't something I learned about back in the day. In my era, retail was king. The majority of my Columbia classmates who didn't end up in management consulting or investment banking went to large retail corporations like Procter & Gamble.

I began my sleuthing, like many people now do, by going straight to Google, where I immediately noticed something unusual: people had a LOT of *emotion* about this business model. Some people were *shouting* their love for Network Marketing from the virtual rooftops, and others were *screaming* that it was a scam. Weird, right? I mean, I've never seen anyone write, "BEING A BARISTA SAVED MY LIFE!" or "DO NOT BECOME AN ACCOUNTANT UNDER ANY CIRCUMSTANCES!" But that was the polarity I found with Network Marketing.

Then I asked Linda a slew of questions, which she patiently answered. *But*, I reasoned, *she was already IN the business, and she had a vested interest in having me there, too.* Therefore I couldn't just take her word.

So, independently, I went deeper, examining the business information offered by her company and a number of other companies who used the same model. I put out personal feelers to see who had intel about this industry. I watched and listened to longtime experts in the field, as well as those who claimed Network Marketing was impossible, immoral, or even illegal.

And what I found was that there was both truth and myth. Fact and fiction.

The more truth and facts I learned, the more I found myself thinking, "Wait. The question really isn't why would someone do this. The question is why *wouldn't* someone do this?" When I finally let myself find and follow the facts, YES was my inevitable answer to Network Marketing, and to Linda.

Since the day I said YES... well, you've already heard a bit of how well it has all worked out for me. Now, obviously, that didn't happen overnight. It happened over time. Which is part of how Network Marketing is designed.

Oh, and by the way, on the day I said YES, did I throw away my pizza crusts, Chardonnay, and chocolate forever? No. Did I become a pushy salesperson? No. Did I have more time in a day? No. I was the same person, one decision later.

Was I still sick? Yes. Was I still scared? Yes. But was I still stuck? Nope. My decision to say YES to this business changed the entire course of my life. And while my four months of doubt and suspicion didn't benefit me, they can benefit you. I did the research. Now you don't have to.

Chapter 3

Network Marketing: What It Is

If anything you read here floats your boat, I don't want you to wait four months, or even four minutes, to say yes to Network Marketing. I am going to tell you the facts, and then you decide what works best for you. You join us on the ride or you don't. Either way, you will feel better informed about a profession that is, like anything Ivy League, steeped in tradition, yet leading in innovation. So here's the scoop:

Network Marketing is:

- A legal, longstanding, yet leading-edge business model.
- A streamlined way of connecting people to products.
- An equal opportunity "opportunity."
- An underexplored answer for work/life balance.
- A low-risk, low-cost way to own your own business.
- A game-changing choice for every generation.

A Legal, Longstanding, Yet Leading-Edge Business Model

Network Marketing has been around for over 100 years. Even before 2020, Network Marketing companies generated over $190 billion in sales worldwide. That's bigger than the NFL, the movie business, and the music business combined. Numerous Network Marketing companies are publicly traded – the largest at over $7 billion. There are one hundred million people involved

22

in this profession. It's real, it's rock solid, and thanks to the explosive growth of online shopping and social media, coupled with changing employment and lifestyle trends, it's one of the fastest growing business models on the planet.

It's innovative – or leading edge – because it allows us to marry the new power of online commerce to our uniquely human ability to bond with others. Of course, Network Marketing companies, like companies in any other industry, must abide by the laws of the countries in which they operate. In the U.S., we follow the Federal Trade Commission (FTC.gov). On top of that, the industry has its own version of the Better Business Bureau – in the U.S., it's the Direct Selling Association (DSA.org). Companies join voluntarily and agree to uphold strict ethical standards.

And, most importantly to anyone considering the profession, Network Marketing companies pay their participants bountifully. This year, Network Marketing Professionals earned more than $76 billion in commissions and overrides. That's over $200 million a day! My company alone paid almost HALF of what it took in last year to its consultants.

A Streamlined Way of Connecting People to Products

As people, we're all already connected, day in and day out, personally and by social media. The Network Marketing model allows us to utilize our connections to profitably share products or services. It connects companies to consumers in a way that benefits both. As professional Network Marketers, we see who in

23

our existing or expanding networks is interested in what we have to offer. When people we're connected to buy what we offer them, we get paid. If they want to make money doing what we do, we show them how, and when our company's products are sold in those networks, we can get paid on those sales, too.

Network Marketing is, at its core, a distribution method. It's a way to get you what you need or want – your STUFF. Network Marketing companies share a part of their revenue with their Consultants (who may also be called Distributors, Associates, or a similar term). Products pass directly from the manufacturer to you, the consumer, via the virtual or actual word of mouth recommendation of the Consultant. Streamlined.

Retail is a distribution method too. It's the one that many of us grew up with. It's our go-to method – where we literally 'go to' a store to get our stuff. In the retail model, once something is made, it goes through many different steps with different middlemen: transportation, warehousing, advertising, marketing, and retail store costs (which include the cost of the retail space rental, the cost to light and heat the space, and the cost of store employees, to name a few). At each step, someone makes a profit. So, the *price* of the product keeps getting marked up, without adding anything to the product's *value*. What does that mean for you as a consumer? WAY higher prices for no higher quality.

Because Network Marketing cuts out the middlemen, the bloat of advertising and retailing costs is avoided. And Network

Marketing rewards the real brand ambassadors – the people who **actually use** the products or services – when they spread the word.

Let's contrast this with what happens when you buy a product promoted with a paid celebrity endorsement. Say, for sh*ts and giggles, Nicole Kidman. Nicole Kidman reportedly earned $4 million a year for her ads with Chanel No. 5 perfume. So far, this has helped her make over $12 million, and helped Chanel No. 5 become the top-selling perfume in the world. But when you spritz on your Chanel No. 5, your friend says, "You smell delish, what is that?" You tell her, "It's Chanel No. 5, isn't it divine?" and she goes and buys some… how much do you earn? Zip. And in fact, *Nicole's* fees are built into the price of *your* perfume. Ouch.

Even when you don't know the face, you're still paying for it. My beautiful friend Kim Starzyk – who is, in addition, an Independent Consultant and VP on my team – also acts in commercials. For one job, she was flown to New Zealand (fun!), and paid a nice five figures to act in a commercial about a bladder control product. Thing is, she's never had a leak in her life.

Audiences watching that commercial probably knew at some level that Kim was just an actor, not an actual sufferer of urinary incontinence. But when they bought the product, they paid for her travel and commercial fees. Markup strikes again.

You might be wondering, what about online brands? Or online sites for retail brands? When you buy something online from a brand that's not a Network Marketing company, a good chunk of the price you're paying is still going to the advertisements that likely brought you to that site in the first place. And someone's definitely making money… but it definitely isn't you.

Life is about choices. As long as consumers know what their choices are costing, they should be free to choose how they spend and on what. But when all is said and done, many of us would rather pay less for the same quality product than not, which Network Marketing allows us to do. And we'd rather buy on the recommendation of someone we actually connect with and relate to than some random actor, salesperson, or paid-to-pose "influencer." Plus, we'd rather participate in something as a business that allows us to earn money by authentically sharing.

An Equal Opportunity "Opportunity"

Anyone can participate in this kind of business. As long as you are 18, there's no one who will tell you you're not old enough, young enough, successful enough, hot enough, or cool enough to be a kickass professional Network Marketer. Conversely, no one will ever tell you that you're too old, too young, too successful, too hot, or too cool to add a Network Marketing business into your life. (YOU may tell yourself these things, but that's on you.)

I'm not being glib here. I am completely passionate about the equal opportunity piece of this industry. When I look at the prejudices that plague not only our employment system but our entire culture – ageism, sexism, ableism, and racial and religious prejudice, to name a few – I'm thrilled to be able to offer an alternative. I'm proud to be part of a profession where everyone has value, and no one can define your worth except you. You don't have to be a certain gender. You don't have to look or act or think a certain way. You don't have to be a star. You don't have to be a saint. You don't have to be able to walk. You don't have to be debt-free or doubt-free. You just have to be yourself, and be committed to learning and earning.

Yusef Seevers, a successful Independent Consultant in my company, says, "*I grew up black and queer in Detroit. Not an easy combo. And I didn't have role models for large scale entrepreneurialism. So I'm inspired to lead by example and show how healthy relationships and a healthy business can work together. For me, as a person of color, saying yes to this industry closes the gap for someone else. Knowing that one day someone I might not even know will see me as a top-level earner, see me doing this in a big, visible way – which might allow them to dream for themselves in a big, visible way – that's key for me.*"

Yin Agbontaen, an Independent Consultant and Regional VP with my company, feels similarly. "*My parents are immigrants – my mom is from China and my dad is from Nigeria. They both worked multiple jobs when I was growing up, and they showed me that you can* create the life you want by working hard. But we didn't get to see each other as much as we would have liked.

"I always saw myself as a boss, running a company, but I have also always wanted to be a mom. And when I have a family, I want to be able to be present for them. So I decided to be an example.

"I love beauty products, and when I was introduced to this company as a college sophomore, I knew immediately that I could partner with them and go to the top. I worked my business on the side during college, and alongside a full-time entertainment job in LA before leaving to commit to doing this full time.

"I see this as a path to generational wealth for typically underserved communities. As women of color, we typically have less access to opportunities, and a bigger pay gap. Not here. I can help show other women how to close the gap, if they're willing to work for it."

An Underexplored Answer for Work/Life Balance

Network marketing is definitely **not** the answer for **everyone**. But it **could** be an answer for almost **anyone**. It gives more choices to more people to create more financial freedom and more time freedom. And it can not only provide ongoing additional revenue, but peace and purpose as well.

One of the few positive aspects of the 2020 COVID-19 crisis was that it forced us to press pause on the everyday. The rats stopped racing. Quarantine demanded that we stop GOING, perhaps to be able to start GROWING.

And that challenging time, despite (or in some cases, because of) its difficulties, allowed many of us the space to see how extremely unbalanced life had become, and to re-evaluate what we REALLY wanted. Some of us realized that we want to create a life with more time for the people who matter to us. Or for talents we feel called to express. Or causes that we feel drawn to. Some of us realized we want to slow down. Others realized how impatient we are to go harder.

Maybe sheltering in place had you appreciating home and wishing you could be there more. Maybe it had you itching to travel... the further the better! If you have kids, maybe you realized that homeschooling made you happy. Maybe it made you nuts (no shame). Maybe you took time to create a bucket list of things you really want to do before you die. Or you created a f*ckit list of things you would RATHER DIE than do. Like perhaps go back to that unfulfilling kind of job from which you were unceremoniously fired or furloughed.

No matter what, millions of people found that, when we stopped the same old, same old, we uncovered a yearning for a "different new, different new" work/life equation.

I don't know what drives you, but whatever it is, having a Network Marketing business might help you restructure your life so that you have more balance – to put in the effort to eventually have both the INCOME and the OUTCOME that you want. It's not the first career path on most people's minds. But it can blow your mind if you let it.

Elizabeth Wright, an Independent Consultant and VP on my team, loves the work/life balance difference this choice has given her: *"Before I started my Network Marketing business, I was working at a mortgage company. The company was an hour and a quarter away, each way, from my house. I was a single mom, frustrated at leaving my young son every day and doing work that felt both unfulfilling and exhausting.*

"When I was introduced to our business, I kept my corporate job until I began making enough that I felt comfortable letting it go... about 2 years in. Now, I could NEVER imagine going back to corporate, because I don't want to. I get to pick up my son at school and attend his events, which I couldn't do before. I also don't have to commute in hellacious traffic ever again! But I had to give my business time to grow and put in the effort required."

Dana Shalit, an Independent Consultant and VP with our company, says: *"I started working at 18, and by age 28, I had a successful event production business in Toronto. I was doing what I thought I needed to with my skill set, taking on every client I could to make ends meet. But I was working 80 hour weeks... can you say burnout? And I didn't see a way out of it. Then I was introduced to this company. In the beginning I found just 5-10 hours a week to squeeze in the extra work. It seemed like even more effort with little financial result at the beginning, however over time, my Network Marketing business* *started to out-earn the amount I was making from my event business. Now, I've stepped away from the relentless pace of the events world entirely. And alongside my Network Marketing business, I run a charitable organization, <u>www.artboundfoundation.com</u>, where I get to invest my time and use my skills for other causes I believe in. So far, we're raised over a million dollars for projects worldwide to strengthen communities, build schools, and provide clean water through creativity and artistic expression."*

A Low Risk, Low Cost Way to Own Your Own Business

SO many people want to be entrepreneurs. It's estimated that two thirds of Americans want to start their own businesses, but only 4% have. Why? Because entrepreneurship – like every other single thing in life – comes with costs and risks. Costs are both metaphorical and actual – but let's just talk about the actual costs here: you'll need to pay for market research, product creation, inventory, insurance, lawyer and accountant bills, website creation... maybe office space or co-working space too. Microbusinesses run about $3,000 to get up and running, while small business start-up fees run most people about $30,000. And clearly, they can cost much more.

And then of course, you'll likely do all the work yourself. You're a one-man band, or rather, a one-man brand. I don't know about you, but I get anxiety thinking about being that. I don't WANT to have to take care of everything myself, especially the stuff I don't LIKE. The making-the-stuff stuff. The back office stuff. The accounting stuff. The delivery stuff. And yup (says the lawyer), the legal stuff.

Alternatively, you might think about buying into a franchise of an already existing brand. If so, I hope you have the dough. Want a Subway franchise? Your estimated total investment will be between $116,600 and $263,150. For a Jamba Juice, you'll need a net worth of at least $300,000, plus liquid capital of $125,000. A McDonald's franchise requires a minimum of $955,000 in "nonborrowed, personal resources" to be considered. Not to mention that you are required to pay a franchise fee on all sales.

And whatever the cost, the risk is real. The U.S. Small Business Administration (SBA) estimates that only 50% of new small businesses survive five years, and about one-third 10 years or longer.

Network Marketing offers a way to "own your own business" with far lower costs and far less risk. It's turnkey. You just say yes, pay an initial joining fee and/or purchase some products, and plug in to the already existing infrastructure and system of your company. The company provides the structure – you just add you.

As professional Network Marketers, we're not actually entrepreneurs; rather, we are "intrapreneurs." An intrapreneur is an entrepreneurial person who chooses to work within the framework of an already existing company. The company takes all the risk, does all the planning, legal and legwork, creates the products or services, and delivers them to end users. It also creates both a system of activity for the intrapreneur to follow, and a compensation plan to let them know what they'll get when they achieve certain benchmarks.

You know you're an intrapreneur if you're excited about creating something that's yours, but don't want to "buy yourself a job" (like most franchisees end up doing), work BY yourself just because you're working FOR yourself (like most small business owners do), or take a major financial dare (like every startup ever).

Intrapreneurship via Network Marketing can be the innovative answer for many to create additional revenue and freedom without overhead or hassles. A Network Marketing intrapreneur puts in a small financial investment (usually between a few hundred and a thousand dollars) and also invests some time in learning, following, and then coaching others in the methods of their company.

Victor So, a member of my team, loved the "Low Risk/Low Cost Business Ownership" factor: *"I'm a Culinary Institute of America graduate and martial artist, and I definitely have an entrepreneurial side. So, in addition to being a full-time chef at a major Manhattan hotel, I created two side businesses. Two big swings, and ultimately – many lessons later – two misses. One was a food truck that, between the price of the truck, supplies, parking in Manhattan, and insurance, cost me $100k! The other was a martial arts studio that* required my dependence on a partner who turned out to be the wrong partner... and cost me "only" $40k. When I found a great Network Marketing company that had products that helped my troubled skin, and heard that I could start my own business for $49, I was IN!"

So did Kezia Hartstein, a VP in our company: "As the former Chief Financial Officer of a large publicly-traded company in my home country of Indonesia, I'm always looking for new business ventures. While living in Canada with my husband and our 4 kids, I used some plastic kitchenware from a Network Marketing company and got curious about the business potential of Network Marketing. I found the industry intriguing – the online, non-inventory business model was so smart. I researched a number of companies, including one with high performance health and beauty products which impressed me so much that I became a client. And I loved the products. But I was truly skeptical that it could generate significant revenue.

"Then we moved to LA, where we invested in a brick and mortar French Café in West Hollywood. Between the build-out and hiring of staff to run it for 3 years, we spent, well, let's just say – in the mid six figures. And then the Café failed.

"That's when I decided to re-consider Network Marketing, but only with this particular company. It met all my criteria. The low start up costs meant no need to tie up a large amount of capital or risk significant loss. The higher end product gave me something I could be proud to share. I liked the simple comp plan and sales-volume based earnings. And so I joined – to "prove" that it could work.

34

"Obviously, I put in significant effort. But every business requires significant effort. And three years later I am happy to say: mission accomplished!"

A Game-Changing Choice for Every Generation

Can we just talk honestly for a minute about how life is trending for, well, every generation in the workforce? *Gen Z*: Fewer jobs than ever available. And many people are saddled with debt – usually from student loans. *Gen Y*: Don't wanna be stuck in one place. Unable to afford to buy homes. Also saddled with debt. *Gen X*: Often have families, but not enough time for them – or anything else. If they make a lot, they can't stop working or they will lose their lifestyle. And very possibly – saddled with debt. *Baby Boomers*: losing their employability in the "regular" job force as they age. Some want to retire but can't afford to, others want to keep working but only on their terms. Oh, and did I mention, this generation is also often saddled with debt – largely credit card debt, with interest that can run up to 26%. **Traditionalists:** for the oldest generation working, most want only to work part time, yet still feel valuable. Social Security isn't cutting it. And over half of this generation is still, yup, saddled with debt.

Network Marketing is age-blind. It can help give anyone, of any generation, the opportunity for more extra money, more flexibility, and more meaning – all of which every generation needs now more than ever.

Consider these five different generations of leaders in my company:

Gen Z – Capri Campeau: *"I found this company when I was 19 and a freshman at a theater conservatory. I had some scholarships, but didn't want to have to borrow to have spending money. I had classes from 9-4, an hour break, then rehearsal or performance 'til around 11 pm – there was no room for a regular part-time job.*

"I love social media. I had a lot of people message me about different online opportunities. But I didn't believe it was a real thing until I met the leaders at my company. Some of them were also doing this alongside college, and some were working actors. I became confident that I could do this alongside school – and also alongside my career afterwards.

"Turns out I don't need to get "hired." I hired myself. And it's working. I feel like I've changed so much. I'm helping people, I'm helping the planet. Being a business owner has given me more confidence as an actor – and more choices too. Now I don't go into an audition desperate to get the role. And I actually book more gigs!"

Gen Y – Bernard Abero: *"I've always been a creative – an actor, dancer, and entertainer. It's important for me to have the freedom to do those things no matter what else I'm doing. In Sacramento, I supported myself as a ballroom dance professional with Arthur Murray Dance Studios – but eventually teaching lost its shine for me, and I thought, maybe I need to get a "normal" job. I went back to school and learned to run a successful insurance business, but it drained my creativity. So I finally said "F it", and moved to Los Angeles to go all in for my dreams.*

To keep flexible for auditions, I took a restaurant job, where, thankfully, one of my customers introduced me to this company.

"I'm the type of person who, if I see and feel a good opportunity, I'm jumping. Here, the vibes were right. I saw other people around me here who were happy, who were positive, who were financially secure. And I decided to SPRINT. This will fuel and fund my passions. I love serving people. But not as a waiter!"

Gen X – Sarah Emanuel: *"I'm entrepreneurial by nature, but I'm also a nurturer – being a present parent to my two young sons is super important to me. My husband and I had agreed that I'd stay home with the kids, and he'd work. But after seven years of my husband working two jobs in the high stress world of high-end restaurants to support us, I wanted to bring him home – at least in the evenings. The kids and I were hardly seeing him, and even though he was earning a lot, we were just getting by – LA is an expensive city! I knew as soon as I heard about this business that I could work it in around the boys' school and sleep times, that it could grow as they did, and that in time, we'd have more time to be together as a family."*

Boomer – Eunice Ray: *"I started my Network Marketing business 17 years ago, when I was 55. I didn't go looking for it – I was busy running a publishing company. In fact I went to a meeting with my daughter because I thought it would be good for HER to check out! And she did join… but when I heard what was possible to create, without having to start when you're 20, I wasn't about to pass it up either! I like keeping busy, I like making money, and this business is perfectly* *positioned as a training ground for the digital economy. For me, every person is a treasure chest, and I am simply looking for the key. Success depends on how many people you can unlock the chest for. Now I tell people, no one can stop you from starting this! Just cannonball in- what do you have to lose?"*

Traditionalist – Jan Dillon: *"After college, I had six different careers, ranging from flight attendant to secretary, administrative assistant, boutique owner, marketing director for a cable tv company, and finally a 20-year stint as a medical staff consultant, helping credential doctors for hospitals. I enjoyed each one, but despite all that work, when I hit my 70s I didn't really have retirement savings. And it was a bit scary, not knowing what I was going to do. I learned about this business from my daughter, and started doing it on the side before I decided to leave my full-time job. I have more comfort now – it gives me a bit of a cushion. And I've never experienced a community like this. So many successful people from different backgrounds. Everyone really cares about everyone."*

So there you have it – the truth about this industry. Network Marketing is here to stay, and for good reason. It's on the rise as an alternative to limited lifestyle and earning options, or as an additional way to make extra money, have more choices, and be of service.

Chapter 4

Network Marketing: What It Isn't

Now that you know clearly what Network Marketing IS, I want you to be just as clear on what it's NOT. Because, if you're going to do this thing, I want to make sure you do it with your arms wide open, and your eyes wide open, too. There are a few persistent misconceptions about Network Marketing, and I want to make sure you understand the truth.

Network Marketing Isn't:

- A pyramid scheme.
- A way to get rich quick.
- A job.
- An either/or.
- A self-driving car.
- A guarantee.

Network Marketing is Not A Pyramid Scheme

"It's a pyramid scheme" was the most common objection I found while researching the Network Marketing profession. Is there any truth to this accusation? Um... no.

Pyramid schemes are by definition ILLEGAL. The U.S. Federal Trade Commission, or FTC, is the organization tasked with protecting consumers from unfair and deceptive practices. They explain that pyramid schemes *"...all share one overriding characteristic. They promise consumers or investors large profits based primarily on recruiting others to join their program, not based on profits from any real investment or real sale of goods to the public."*

By contrast, Network Marketing companies are by definition LEGAL. The FTC says that Network Marketing companies, *"...unlike [pyramid] schemes... have a real product to sell. More importantly, [they] actually sell their product to members of the general public. [They] may pay commissions to a long string of distributors, but these commissions are paid for real retail sales, not for new recruits."*

The FTC gives specific warning signs to differentiate illegal pyramid schemes from legit Network Marketing companies. In a pyramid scheme, you're offered extravagant promises about your earning potential. You're subjected to high pressure "act now" sales tactics. Or you're told that the "real" way to make money is by recruiting new distributors. Or you have to buy more products than you use or can resell, just in order to stay active or get bonuses and rewards.

OK. So, if Network Marketing companies are NOT pyramid schemes, why do so many people wrongly say that they are?

Well, a couple of reasons. First, what some people mean when they say "pyramid" is simply that more than one person can make money when a single sale occurs. And that makes them somehow suspicious instead of excited. As if life is a zero-sum game, where if you're making some money, someone else shouldn't also be making some money. Yeah, no. Win-win actually exists.

And then there's the pyramid shape. Incorrect presumptions are usually on the order of, "only one person (or a few people) can make it to the top." Or, "if you don't get in early you can't succeed." Or, "the people at the top are taking advantage of the people on the bottom."

Network Marketing is, if anything, the inverse of a pyramid. Yes, you'll start out "at the bottom" as a newbie, signed up to someone who has been there longer and is therefore metaphorically "higher up." They may even make money when you make money. And that's great – do what they do and you'll have what they have. However, anyone can start "at the bottom" and work their way "to the top." And there's no limit to the number of people who can be at the top.

By the way, have there been some illegal pyramid schemes attempting to masquerade as legal Network Marketing companies? Yes. For example, the nutrition company Vemma, which was shown to have falsely represented that their members were likely to earn up to $50,000 a week, when in fact most earned $12,000 a year or less. Definitely "liar, liar, pants on fire" behavior. And Vemma was shut down by the FTC.

Bad business is done in many industries, but that doesn't mean any whole industry is bad. Wells Fargo Bank, for example, created millions of fraudulent checking and savings accounts without customer consent. Yet we all still bank, and some still bank at Wells Fargo, after it paid a *three billion dollar fine* and promised to change its ways. So, before you give up a potential additional revenue stream with a Network Marketing company, do some fact checking based on the specific company and the people involved.

Network Marketing Is Not a Get Rich Quick Game

As noted in the FTC info above, if someone tells you that, with their company, you can make six figures in six weeks, or even six months, please say, "No thanks." Network Marketing is a BUSINESS opportunity, and businesses take time and tenacity to build. They do not spring fully formed as if from the head of Zeus.

Your business will be built ...day by day... conversation by conversation... order by order... business partner by business partner.

If you say yes to building a business in Network Marketing, say yes knowing that in order to see the results, it will take time. Not forever, but some actual amount of time. Obviously, there is work involved (i.e. *effort*... **I mean, come on, it's a business**), but it's up to you when you do it, how you do it, with whom, how much you enjoy it, and how much you make.

Network Marketing Is Not a Job

A job is a group of duties, tasks, or responsibilities for which someone pays you a certain amount, guaranteed. Most are the typical straight time-for-money trades – work a certain number of hours, get paid a certain amount.

For some people, the fact that Network Marketing is NOT a job is the reason they say YES, and YIPPEE. They don't want to be defined or hemmed in by someone else telling them when or where they have to work or how much they can earn.

Network Marketing Is Not an Either/Or

A lot of people think the concept is, "Either I'll do Network Marketing OR I'll keep my job." Nuh-uh. Almost any Network Marketing professional will tell you that they built their business alongside their original job... or in this economy, their jobs. Network Marketing is designed to be part-time, either for the long term, or until such time as you are making enough that you can decide whether you want to stop any full time or other part-time jobs you might have.

So, if you have a full-time job, please don't start a Network Marketing business expecting that it will quickly – or perhaps ever – yield as much revenue. However, do start knowing that given time, intention, and attention, Network Marketing can be the add-on that makes everything else flow better, and that it's *possible* (NOT guaranteed) that at some point in the future, it could provide the same amount, or more.

Network Marketing is Not a Self-Driving Car

The great news is that Network Marketing is a vehicle that can get you literally wherever you want to go in your life. But the other news is, you still have to fill the tank, learn the rules of the road, and put pedal to the metal.

Network Marketing can be for anyone, but it's definitely not for everyone. Lots of people would rather not bet on themselves. They'd rather not take on the personal growth required to be successful. They'd rather feel stuck or dissatisfied than get into that strange new vehicle. However, if you have even the slightest inspiration to experiment, I suggest a test drive.

Network Marketing is Not a Guarantee

It only works if you do. There is work that's required – both outer and inner. Business skills *and* self-development are essential for success. There are no guarantees to our time on this planet, as we all know. There are only options, opportunities, risks and rewards.

And I will tell you right now, most people who start a Network Marketing business DON'T reach the top level of their company earnings-wise. That doesn't show that Network Marketing doesn't work. What it does show is that people sometimes quit, are uncoachable, don't have a big reason *why* they're doing the business, or are simply not committed. Again, totally ok. But mostly – and this is REALLY important – it shows that, for the majority of people, being at the top is not their aim. Lots of folks are happy just having *a little something more* than they had before.

So now you are clear on what Network Marketing is and isn't. Let's focus next on how smart Network Marketing is – and why you might say it's Ivy League by design.

Chapter 5

A Smart Business for Smart People

Ivy Leaguers are known for being smart. Smart people outsource. Smart people prepare for impact. Smart people get the best deals. Smart people find solutions. Smart people capitalize on their power as consumers and as influencers. Smart people leverage their time. Network Marketing allows anyone to be Ivy League smart, because through this one business vehicle, you can do all these smart things at once.

Consider these Ivy League Tips ( ) while you make your decision whether to start a Network Marketing business.

 Utilize Built-in Outsourcing.

No one's great at everything, and with Network Marketing, we don't have to be. Outsourcing (finding an outsider to take care of something so you don't have to) is a massive trend in business. Companies outsource research, design, facilities management, supply chain management, accounting, content writing, website development, and legal documentation, among other things. It's Ivy League to outsource what you're least talented at, or least interested in, because it allows you to focus on your strengths. Lots of people try to start their own businesses, don't (or can't afford to) outsource enough, and burn out.

Network Marketing is smart because it's designed KNOWING most that people don't want to do it all. With this business model, you get to easily bring outsourcing into your personal business.

For example, my company has over 250 products – and I didn't have to invent, design, test, package, or ship them. All that "detailia," including that eye-crossing back office stuff? Done for me. Gorgeous product photos? Done for me. Pre-made email templates? Done for me. People just order products from my company, online, at *my* company-created website. The great stuff they want gets delivered to their doors, and I get my thank you check.

 Prepare for Impact.

Sh*t happens. It's inevitable. Whether it's an accident, a divorce, a dry spell, a work change, a natural disaster, or a pandemic... something's coming down the road. And it's going to impact you physically, mentally, spiritually. According to a recent study, 40% of the people in the U.S. don't have an extra $400 saved in case of an emergency; for instance, an unexpected medical expense. Which is pretty bad when you learn that the average "surprise bill" for an emergency room visit has risen to $628.

And even if you avoid the emergency room or live in a country where your health care is free, life's getting more expensive, not less. The job market is less and less stable. Income inequality and debt are UP. WAY UP. Savings and retirement accounts are DOWN. WAY DOWN. Network Marketing is a way to have a smart "in case of impact" financial option already rolling.

For a smart person, I wasn't very smart before I joined my Network Marketing company. I had one main source of income (mistake number one) and I had the hubris or inexperience to think I'd be fine – and so would everyone else in my family-- no matter what (mistake number two). Hence my panic when I got sick and the music business dried up while the economy crashed all at the same time. Lesson learned. Now I get to show other people how they can avoid making the same mistakes.

My smart teammate Samantha Geraci-Yee was prepared for impact: *"I followed my passion and became a professional opera singer. I was sought after as a vocalist, and booked new jobs consistently. However, I didn't make enough from those jobs to get ahead, or even get by, and I got really tired of the stress of waiting tables and having mind-numbing "show up at this shift" gigs. When I began working with our Network Marketing company, it was just to get to a place of having a little more financial breathing room.*

"Then, the unthinkable happened. My mother, who lived across the country, was diagnosed with a virulent recurrence of the breast cancer she thought she had beaten.

Because I now had a mobile, phone-based Network Marketing business, I was able to pick up on a moment's notice, move where I was needed, and be available every day to the most important person in my life, at the most important time. And because I had built my business to a significant level, my income didn't disappear. In the year before my mom passed, my clients kept buying products, my team kept working, and I maintained my earnings. I am forever grateful that I said YES to Network Marketing!"

 Get The Best Deals.

Network Marketing companies typically give brand representatives big discounts on their own products. Who doesn't want that? 'Nuf said.

 Find Solutions.

It's not a secret: the majority of people are experiencing problems. Too little job security, too little financial stability, or too little time to do what they want, where they want, with whom they want. Not-as-smart people bitch with friends, numb themselves out with their favorite bad habit, from devices to drinking, or just give up and surrender to the "oh, well, what can you do?" mentality.

Smart people find solutions, even when they're outside the box. If you're smart, you'll consider Network Marketing as a potential solution. A solution that could stop you from suffering through a life by default, and begin to build a life by design.

 Utilize Your Power as a Consumer.

We all do two things regularly: we shop for stuff, and we share what we like. We shop for candles, cruises, lipstick, wine, TV shows, cars, music, whatever. And when we like something, we share it with other people. Think of every restaurant, salon, movie, new song, or clothing brand you have ever recommended to a friend. That's word of mouth marketing. Shop and share. And we all do it... for free.

As professional Network Marketers, we simply shop and share, too, but with a twist – we can get paid. We shop a particular brand, we like it, and we share it. We show people why, where, and how to shop for that brand, and get paid when they buy it. Simple. And we share the 'shop and share' business model, so if people want, we show them how to do this and get paid for it, too. Simple.

Plus, we all vote with our dollars. We declare, with every purchase, not just that we like a product, but that we value the ethics and policies of the company behind it. Network Marketing allows us to be part of a volunteer army of career consumers who have decided to support a particular company that aligns with who we are. We choose our brand, use our brand, and spread the word to others – amplifying our voices through our consumer choices.

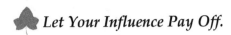

Let Your Influence Pay Off.

We all influence others, and Network Marketing is a smart way to potentially let your influence increase your affluence. For most people, Network Marketing is a way to make a little extra money, which is always smart. And for the right person, a Network Marketing business can be a plan B, or even a plan A. It can protect you, and provide you flexibility and peace of mind.

And, more important, because it's a business you can build part-time, you can do it anytime, anywhere, alongside your existing commitments. I know people who have built their businesses on carpool lines, on treadmills, in hospital waiting rooms, or standing in line at the grocery store.

Leverage Your Time.

Time – unlike, say, solar power- is a non-renewable resource: you only get so much of it in your life. Which makes it even more precious. In a traditional job, you are simply trading your time for money – whether you earn an annual salary or are being paid by the hour. You, just you, yourself, have to show up and do all the work required for YOUR job. You're "on the clock," literally or figuratively, and there will always be a cap on your earnings.

Lack of time leveraging is what makes a lot of successful professionals **time-poor**. Surgeons who get paid per procedure.

Advisors who charge by the hour. Receptionists. Trainers. Physical Therapists. Broadway performers. You get the picture.

Network Marketing is, again, different by design. Time leveraging is built into the model: you can make money not just from your own efforts, but others' efforts as well. When you coach and train others to do what you do, you receive a piece of the sales value of your collective efforts (and of those they teach, and those *they* teach, etc.).

You get paid on the efforts of many… **starting with yourself, of course**. Everyone is buying a little, sharing a little, working a little, and everyone can earn a lot.

To me, time leveraging is the most brilliant – that is, the most Ivy League – thing about Network Marketing. Why? Because it allows you to make more of the time you DO have, while still creating revenue, and not just from your own efforts.

Roni Geva Orlina, a fellow National VP with my company, says: *"I started my Network Marketing business at 25, when I was a struggling sketch writer/actor in Chicago. I had six part time jobs that often got in the way of my going to auditions. Through my business, I learned how to do short presentations for 6-10 people at a time, and earn extra money in a few hours a week. When I signed a few fellow actors onto my team, and taught them how to do what I was doing, I got paid not only on the results of my efforts, but theirs too.*

"Within a year, I was able to "fire" my six bosses. And because I had more time, I could go to those auditions. Very quickly, I booked a

show, got my Equity card, and was nominated for a "Jeff" Award (the Chicago equivalent of a Tony). Apparently, all I needed was more time!

"Fast forward – well okay, not THAT fast – I got married, started a family, brought more clients and consultants onto my team, rose to the top of the company, and moved to LA.

"There – again, because I had more time – I co-created, wrote and starred in my own web series, which was nominated for an Emmy! I always say – doing Network Marketing didn't get me nominated for an Emmy, but it sure paved the way in giving me the flexibility to follow my dreams. Best side hustle ever."

CHECK-IN TIME

I've presented a lot of information here, and I'm a big believer in processing. Take a few minutes right now, and answer a few of these key questions for yourself:

Are you currently leveraging your time, or trading your time for money?

_____

_____

How many brands and companies do you regularly "promote" for free by recommending them to others, wearing their logos, or sharing their sites?

_____

_____

Do you like getting the best deals? Or is retail still your go-to?

_____

_____

What's a challenge in your life for which you're seeking a solution?

_____

_____

Are you financially prepared for unexpected events, both in your personal world, and in the world at large?

_____

_____

If you keep doing exactly what you're doing right now, where will you be in 5 years, especially financially – and how will that feel?

_____

_____

If something should happen to the main source of income in your household, how long can you comfortably rely on your savings?

_____

_____

Chapter 6

Yeah, But...

I've given you a lot of good reasons why you **could** start a Network Marketing business. However, starting a business is a personal decision. You're a person. And people are funny – we'd often rather doubt, doubt, doubt than just dive in.

By the time we reach adulthood, we're well-versed in the fine art of objection, or what one of my delightful mentors, *Financial Stress Reduction* author and coach Chellie Campbell, calls "**YEAH, BUT.**" The truth is, we tend to "**YEAH, BUT**" *most* new ideas when they're initially presented. Why? Well, first off, we don't want to look like idiots, and objections make us feel clever. Second, "**YEAH, BUT**" gives us an excuse to close the door on possibility or accountability. Objections can be legit, but all too often they are simply **fear masquerading as fact.**

Here are the most common **YEAH, BUTs** about Network Marketing.

"Yeah, but... I don't have enough time."

This is one of the most common *"yeah, buts."* It *might* be true, but is it *really*? Do you truly not HAVE the time, or are you simply not willing to MAKE the time? The good news – and the bad news – is that we all have the same 1440 minutes in a day. What we DO with those minutes is a series of choices and priorities. Yes, we may have some ironclad obligations – maybe a day job, child care, or elder care. However, we ALL have *small segments of time* that *we can choose to use* to build a side business *if it's important enough to us.*

I learned the 1440 concept from one of my company's top leaders, Ashley Strong, who built her business in a very time-disciplined way, reaching our top level in less than HALF the average time of 5 years, WHILE she was an Active Duty Master Sergeant in the U.S. Air Force working a minimum of 60 hours a week.

How? Well first, she decided building a business was WORTH IT TO HER. Then, she woke up a little earlier, and went to bed a little later. She became intentional about fitting in a few texts here, a phone call there – on the way to work, at lunch, on the way home, after dinner. She learned how to lead group discussions as often as possible. She calendared in time for her business and stuck to her dates with herself. Doing this, she rose to our company's highest level in 21 months.

If she can do this, what's your excuse? Or any of ours? **When we want something ENOUGH, "busy" disappears**. As a general rule, *we MAKE time for what moves us. We FIND time for what's important. And we GIVE UP less important things to GET what we care about most.*

Let's face it – a lot of us are spending time – or, more accurately, wasting time – in ways that don't add up in the bigger picture.

That new Netflix series may be fun, but watching it won't pay your bills. Neither will going online to "check one thing" and climbing back out of the rabbit hole a half an hour (or an hour and a half) later. And every minute lost fretting about bills, personal dramas, or the current state of the world? That's time you could have been using to change your life with Network Marketing.

🍃 *"Busy" can be a truth or an excuse. Decide what's most important to you and invest your time appropriately.*

"Yeah, but I don't have enough money."

The money "**yeah, but,**" like the time "**yeah, but,**" is often not a matter of literally not having money, but of what you CHOOSE to do with the money you DO have. Many people with this *yeah, but* are not thinking about the big picture potential benefits of a Network Marketing business – they are simply giving a knee jerk response because they are stuck in a feeling of lack.

However, feelings aren't facts. According to the DSA, the average required Network Marketing start up kit fee in the U.S. is $82.50 (yes, you read that right). Usually a company will also recommend – *not require* – that you purchase a few initial products for yourself, and if you take that route, you might want to budget a few hundred dollars to do so. Altogether, less than many people pay for a cell phone.

My company, for example, requires only $49 for your e-store, free mentorship and bountiful online training, as well as a 35-50% discount on all of your own products for a year. And we recommend, *but don't require,* newbies to purchase one or more of our bestsellers for healthy living, inside and out. If you follow our training, you can (*no guarantees)* start turning a profit within the first few months of your business, while also enjoying our products yourself, at a substantial discount, with a 90-day money back guarantee.

Look, I do live in reality. I know that the majority of Americans (78% actually… *including* those making $100k a year) are living paycheck to paycheck, or perhaps more accurately in the current economic climate, "pray check to pray check." You *might* have to take time to save enough, or wait until your next funds come in, or even create a Kickstarter to start a Network Marketing business. And if so, that's fine.

But if you simply FEEL you can't afford to start a business, look at what you're spending elsewhere. See where you're getting a potential future bang for your buck, and where you're just spending instead of truly investing. Can you really 'not afford' to start your Network Marketing biz, or can you not afford NOT to?

🍃 *Ask, "Is this an opportunity I can't afford to take, or an opportunity I can't afford to miss?"*

"Yeah, but I'm not a salesperson."

Phew! Neither am I... if by "salesperson" you mean one of those pushy, rude folks who badger you relentlessly, hawking useless crap, and don't take no for an answer. Yet sales are occurring in my business every single day. People are buying, so technically, I'm selling.

Sales are everywhere. If you're a parent, you "sell" your kids on everything from going to sleep at a reasonable hour to the importance of flossing. If you're a partner, you "sell" your preferences on everything from division of labor to what next to binge-watch. With friends and family, you "sell" your points of view. In work, at play, online, and IRL, you are continually "selling" – your positions, your truths, your beliefs. It's part of human nature.

And you're not just selling concepts...you, yes you, are actually selling STUFF... for companies. Every time you wear a bag or a hat or a shirt with a logo... every time you drive your car... every time you recommend a movie, you're "selling" what you're wearing, using, or watching. You're just not getting any thank-you checks.

The bad rap about salespeople is that they're somehow inauthentic. And certainly, there are some inauthentic people in sales – just like there are some inauthentic people in politics, in the press, in courtrooms, and in corporate culture.

However, in my experience, Network Marketing is a chance to be 100% authentic. We in this profession will happily tell you that YES, we purchase, use, and enjoy our brand, because we see real value in it, and YES, we invite you to do so as well. If you see what we see, you can purchase through us, and YES – it's not a secret – we will make some money from the company for introducing you to them. Plus, if you want to, YOU can have the exact same opportunity to make money as well.

Here's a good way to look at sales: sharing, recommending, and serving. I authentically share information, inspiration, insight, options, opportunities, and support. I serve people by letting them know what I have that might fit their needs. I show them where to shop, and I recommend they do so. If something I have is of interest, people sell *themselves* on whether it's right for them. If THAT's a salesperson, then I'm proud to be one. And someday you might be, too.

🍂 *Explore your prejudices about selling. Embrace the truth that we all "sell" one another, and ourselves, on the things we believe in. Consider selling yourself on the idea that selling is normal, natural, and of service to others.*

"Yeah, but I don't know enough people."

Highly unlikely. If you're an average American, you know 600 people. Even if you're not average, you actually might know more people than you realize. I mean, if I told you I'd give you

$10,000 for every name of someone you know right now, I bet you could likely list a LOT. Yes, or yes?

So let's start with the PEOPLE YOU KNOW RIGHT NOW. If you live somewhere, work somewhere, work out somewhere, worship somewhere, eat somewhere, shop somewhere, or shoot the breeze somewhere, you know people right now. If you're in a family, a neighborhood, a book club, a sports league, or a service organization, you know people right now.

Next, there are the PEOPLE YOU USED TO KNOW. When you think about it, in your entire life, you've met a LOT of people: schoolmates, teachers, neighbors, friends, servers, business associates, people you've prayed with, people you've played with, people you met at a wedding, a party, a brunch, actual friends, online friends, whomever. And even if they've been out of your life for a while, any one of them could be the one who changes your life. (My mentor Linda has the largest Canadian business in our company because of ONE message she sent to ONE person she hadn't spoken to in 15 years.)

And that's just people from your past and present. Then there are the PEOPLE YOU WILL MEET. Meeting new people is a learned skill. In any good Network Marketing company, your mentors will show you how to reach out to, and authentically connect with, new people. In other words, teach you to be an *intentional networker*.

Here's where it gets fun: every single person you know or knew or will meet, knows, used to know, and will meet lots of other people too. And you can ask every person in your network to refer their people to you. So, between all these categories, it's super likely that YOU KNOW, KNEW, or WILL MEET enough people.

When you are intentional about meeting people, and about asking them whether what you're offering is something that might serve them <u>or the people they know,</u> your world becomes exponentially bigger. Your potential consumer and consultant bases can expand endlessly.

And so, by the way, can the richness of your life. So, if your mind starts *"yeah, butting"* you with "I don't know enough people," you can very politely tell it to shut up.

🍀 *Distrust your guesstimates. Open your contact list, look at your social media, and count the number of people there. Know that this number is enough to begin to build a successful Network Marketing Business.*

"Yeah, but my cousin (or neighbor or friend) tried it and it didn't work for them."

Can't argue with that. The question is, "Why?" Maybe they didn't choose a company with which they truly aligned (*it happens*). Maybe their mentor was AWOL (*it happens*). But maybe they said yes and did no (*it happens... a lot*). Maybe they weren't patient (*it happens more often than not*). Maybe they didn't follow the instructions their company laid out for them (*it happens with stunning regularity*). Maybe they weren't coachable (*it happens even more frequently*). Maybe they gave it their some and not their all (*it happens all the time*). Maybe they let their fear get in the way of their fire (*it happens most of all, and is the root cause of almost every failure.*)

The reasons vary. But one thing is for sure – THEY AREN'T YOU. If you believe in yourself, and you believe in the company you choose, your chances of success are a LOT better than theirs.

When I hear this *yeah, but*, I might say, "Wow, sorry their experience didn't work out. Do you happen to know why?" And the person I'm asking *might* know, or think they do. As likely as not, though, the reason someone gives as to why their Network Marketing business didn't work out might not be the **real** reason. And the real reason might be hidden, even to the person who failed. Aunt Katherine may be an annoying know-it-all. Neighbor Ryan might have no social skills. Friend Justin might have his own self-imposed glass ceiling for success.

If you have this *yeah, but*, I suggest you educate yourself about the people who have succeeded in this type of business. Odds are that whoever invited you to check out their Network Marketing business will have some great examples from their own company. And there are MANY more industry-wide.

Here are two places to find excellent examples:

Eric Worre's *Network Marketing Pro* podcasts (see www.networkmarketingpro.com) and Richard Bliss Brooke's *Network Marketing Heroes* and *Global Influencer* series (see www.richardbrooke.com).

🍀 *Decide for yourself. If someone you know hasn't succeeded at Network Marketing, parse what happened from why it happened. Ask yourself, "In what way am I different from those who didn't succeed?"*

"Yeah, but I tried it myself and it didn't work for me."

If that's your story, it's DEFINITELY TRUE. AND it's also definitely in the past. Before you say, "…and that's why I'm never doing Network Marketing again," look honestly into what happened and why. Maybe you didn't authentically give a hoot about the company's products, or it wasn't the right time for you, or you didn't receive enough support from your mentors, or have the right mindset. Then ask yourself, *could it be different this time?*

If you were in a situation that left you drained, could you imagine what it would be like if you felt energized? If you were feeding yourself negative thoughts about the outcome, could you imagine what could happen if you shifted into a state of positive expectation?

Is there a **"WHY"** right now that is calling you to show up differently for yourself**?**

Remember, you get to write the story of your life, and the pen is literally in your hand (or, the keyboard is at your fingertips). You can stay stuck in your old story, or you can decide to create a different future. Not saying Network Marketing is definitely for you. Just saying that history isn't destiny.

Don't let your past define you. Be honest with yourself and open up to changing your story. Learn from the past, live in the present, and claim a future you love.

"Yeah, but most people don't make much money at these kinds of things."

You know what, you're 100% right. So, let's explore why. The numbers don't lie ... or do they? Well yeah, actually – or more precisely, they seriously mislead, for four reasons.

First off, the numbers of people not making much money include the huge group of people who join Network Marketing companies simply to be glorified discount consumers, and don't ever take step one for the business side.

My mom, for example. She has been buying a great tea and energy powder that she swears by, from a major Network Marketing company, for over 30 years. She never wanted to have clients or business partners – she was, and is, just obsessed with her tea and energy powder. But technically, she's listed as one of the company's over 300,000 distributors. Could she hang out her shingle any day? Yes. Has she? No. Does the $0 earned next to her name each year bring down the average earnings per distributor of this company? You bet.

Secondly, the numbers also include the *dabblers* – the large number of people who "try" the business but fail. The biggest reason someone fails is that they weren't ever really committed to succeeding. For many, it was just a passing fancy, a wish, or even a strong desire – for a minute, or a week, or a month. Just like most people who join gyms in January don't end up working out in December – or even April. They cared, just not that much. I can personally name 100 people who joined my team and excused themselves almost right away.

Thirdly, the numbers include those who claim to be committed yet aren't taking the specific steps their companies lay out to succeed. Which is a lot of folks. Or, sometimes, they're actually not spiritually ready to succeed. They want to, but don't feel, at some level, like they deserve to. So they go through the motions without going through the correct emotions. And they don't get the biggest results. In both cases, it's impossible to tell how many people are being counted in as business builders when in fact they have already counted themselves out.

Finally, and perhaps most importantly, the numbers include the many people who don't ever want to be superstars or max out the compensation plan. They are actually content to simply have a small business – to earn something, but not a lot.

The real question is not what most people do, but what YOU do. Every Network Marketing company has a compensation plan and a way to grow to the top. Some people are making a lot of money. Will you be one of them? Are you someone who will say yes, work your business like a real business, stretch and grow in the places you need to, and follow a plan until you succeed?

 The numbers are misleading. They don't measure desire, dedication, or commitment. The true test is not what most people make or fail to make, but what is possible to make, and what you decide to make. If you commit to making a significant amount in your Network Marketing business, you can.

"Yeah, but I'm too old, young, educated, uneducated, shy, loud, differently-abled."

Nope. False. No one can tell you that you are too anything (or not enough of something) for this business. Network Marketing is the most level playing field ever created. If you are looking only at one, some, or even the majority of people who have succeeded, you are limiting your vision.

What's that Henry Ford quote? "Whether you believe you can do a thing or not, you are right." **Truth.** No ifs, ands, or **yeah, buts** about it.

🍂 *Remember that Network Marketing is by design an equal opportunity opportunity. If you are telling yourself it's not, chances are 100% that you're BS-ing yourself.*

"Yeah, but people are going to judge me."

Wait... did you think they weren't ALREADY judging you? Don't make me snort! And if they're thinking you're crazy for doing this Network Marketing thing, <u>*newsflash – that's*</u> <u>*about*</u> <u>*them, not about you.*</u> It needs to fall into the "what you think of me is none of my business" category. As my great friend and mentor Sue Cassidy, who has the largest international business in my company, says, *"Would these people pay your mortgage? And would they pay your hospital bills? If not – why are you giving your power to them?"*

This from someone with PLENTY of people ready to judge her. When she started her business, Sue was a stay-at-home celebrity mom, instrument-rated pilot and private plane owner, and multi-platinum songwriter known for her philanthropic work. There were a LOT of eyes on her.

Thanks to Sue, I learned to pull back from the pushback. And you can too. Just decide not to let the fact that people might JUDGE you STOP you. And if the people you know keep judging you instead of loving you, you might want to consider changing up who you are hanging out with.

Being a professional Network Marketer, you will hear a lot, see a lot, and learn a lot about what people believe. Sometimes they believe things that aren't real, are vastly exaggerated, or just plain incorrect. Sometimes they project a massive load of their own fears and doubts onto you. But the only way these things can affect you is IF YOU BELIEVE THEM TOO. Also, remember, judgment cuts both ways. Some people – MORE AND MORE people – will judge you POSITIVELY. Some people are already into this business model and will say BRAVO. Some people will be flippin' GRATEFUL that you offered them a solution to a challenge they were having. Some people will be DELIGHTED that you have decided to bring a product or a service into their lives that they can use and enjoy. And some will be THRILLED at the chance to build a business for themselves.

And if you start a Network Marketing business and can't find a rabid cheerleader, I volunteer. Just email me at cheermeonamy@ivyleaguenetworkmarketing.com and I will send you a rousing huzzah!

You, and only you, decide your destiny. Other people's opinions won't pay your bills, or empower you, or help you sleep easy. YOU be the judge.

Chapter 7

Find Your Fit

Have you dealt with any **yeah, buts** and decided that the Network Marketing business model is up your alley? Great! Now the question becomes which of the thousands of companies is the best one for you? All Network Marketing companies are not created alike any more than all of *any* kind of company are created alike. Target is not Saks Fifth Avenue. Whole Foods is not 7/11.

Here's how to Ivy League your decision:

Choose a company that's right for you in terms of its history, leadership, products or services, vision, compensation plan, and culture. Somewhere you will be AT HOME. Network Marketing is all about relationships – starting with yours. You are looking for the right relationship between you, a company, its products, and your clan of fellow business owners. You will be spending significant time with each. So put on your Ivy League thinking cap, and just as importantly, your Ivy League feeling cap, and assess the following key issues:

How Long Has This Company Been in Business?

Substantially more than half of ALL new companies – Network Marketing or not – fail in their first ten years. If you love risk and the adrenaline rush that goes with it, be the outlier who goes with a young company. However, if you feel – like most people – that life is risky enough without attaching your fortunes to a less than proven brand, look for a company that's been in business a longer time.

Who's in Charge?

What do you know about management and the way they do business? What are their credentials? And how accessible are they? Ideally, you want a company whose CEO/Founder and top sales, marketing, legal, operations, and product development staff have significant experience in the Network Marketing arena and are respected in the industry. You want to know that they have been able to navigate growth and change. And you want designated high-level corporate staff who communicate regularly and openly with the company's field of consultants.

Julie Fedeli found her fit through a CEO/Founder, whose nutritional supplements changed her life.

"I started out in the high-powered, high stress NYC finance world, but realized my heart wasn't in it. So I did a deep dive into meditation and the healing arts, completing a 4-year training with renowned Physicist/Ph.D. and energy healer Barbara Brennan. Eventually I became one of the first alternative medical healers in Chicago. But after I had my son, I was diagnosed with a health challenge, and I remained ill for nine years. I lost all the hair on the top of my head. I couldn't think straight. I was exhausted. It was all I could do to focus the little energy I had on making sure my son was OK.

Then, randomly, I connected with an MD/Ph.D. who shared information with me about a product line. She started sending me emails, but I ignored them for a year. Then – when I finally stopped deleting her messages – I fell in love with these products.

And though I hadn't been looking for a business, when I realized how much better I was feeling, AND just as importantly, that there must be MANY other women with similar issues looking to feel better, I couldn't not share what I knew. I felt like I'd cracked the code and needed to show other women how to do that too."

Products or Services?

Are they you-ish? Make sure you find what the company has to offer personally useful or enjoyable. The more you believe the services or products actually do work and produce results that uplevel your own life, the more authentic you will be recommending them to others. I am not saying you need to be a service or product junkie, but you DO need to find them truly excellent, and actually believe that you are doing something that's a net positive by offering them to others. Extra points, of course, for being honestly obsessed, and not being able to imagine living without them.

Joshua Figg found his fit with a toast-worthy product that held a special place in his heart.

"I spent part of my twenties in wine country in Oregon and got a great education in, and appreciation for, red wine. Eight years ago, I was working in elementary special education, and looking to supplement my income. I knew people in a number of different Network Marketing

companies, and I thought the concept was great, but none of the products lit me up. So I decided to do a little online research. This company was one of the first that popped up. I remember that jolt of delight, and thinking, "This can't be real! How could I not already know about this?

"Like many people, I was initially skeptical that a Network Marketing company could have truly high quality products. But when I learned about our winemaker's extensive, award-winning background, and tasted the wines for myself, I was hooked.

"Now I work my Network Marketing business full time. I love it! And I'm so gratified when guests at tastings say to me, 'You know, I've never hosted an in-person party before, but I'm booking with you!'"

Mia Goswick found her fit with a company that features nail polish strips:

"I've painted my nails since I was little, and I used to go for manicures regularly – it's totally part of who I am. I'd been looking for a business I could do alongside school. I looked into a Network Marketing company for clothing, but for me it was too much of an investment. Then I got sent a sample of these strips and was just blown away. I thought to myself, "I'm never going back to the salon again!"

"Since I was under 20, and my dad is the CEO of a company, I made him a business plan. He thought it made so much sense that he even gave me the $129 it cost me to start!

"This company's been a game changer for me. It's easy for me to share because I'm my own advertisement, and it's such a WOW to other people, especially to people who have never experienced these products before. Clients are so happy, and my team is really growing!"

And while we're on the subject of products, is there a minimum amount, or autoship, you're required to purchase every month? If so, do you enjoy the products so much that you'd be good with getting them every single month in the amount you're required? If not, maybe you're the kind of person who doesn't like to be told what to do, or maybe it's a red flag that you're not really excited about the product. One option is to avoid the whole issue by choosing a company – like mine and a number of others – that doesn't require you to personally buy anything in particular – autoship or not.

What's Their Mission?

Does what this company stands for get your blood pumping? Alignment is key. Mission statements range from a company "creating a world where everyone can access legal protection and everyone can afford it" (LegalShield) to a financial services company here to "help families become properly protected, debt-free, and financially independent" (Primerica) to one that believes "clothes can change lives" (Cabi) to a coffee/weight loss company that aims to "help people live healthier lives one cup at a time" (Javita Coffee). You will be the one on the front lines, being the face of this brand. Make sure that what lights them up lights you up.

Christy Dove found her fit with a company whose mission – safety – aligned with hers.

"I was a firefighter/EMT for 25 years. My day job is working for Toyota in their environmental health and safety division. I have a degree in Occupational Safety and Health, and I make sure what's done at my company is OSHA compliant.

"I'd never done this kind of business before, and I swore I never would. But when I heard about this company – I felt I just HAD to!

"I was at an event with the Fire Department where this company also had a booth, and one of their reps gave us a catalog. When I saw that this company had products that helped people protect themselves from danger – everything from stun guns and pepper spray to identity theft prevention – I felt compelled to call that rep. So much so that when she didn't call back, I made it my business to find someone else at the company and sign up!

"My background fits hand-in-glove with this. If I can save one person, it's worth it. Some people who use our products are concerned about domestic abuse. I'm not a survivor of that, but I know everyone needs protection. As a runner, I know we all want to be safe in our own neighborhoods. And not just from people... I've been bitten twice by dogs! Our products make it possible for ANYONE to feel safer. You have to have a passion for what you do, and with this company, I DO!"

Irene Anderson found her fit with a financial services company whose mission dovetailed with her values and experience.

"I'm a VP with a leading firm that offers families and individuals financial planning, insurance, and investment services. I got my start

on Wall Street, at JP Morgan Private Banking, and I spent 15 years there. But ultimately it wasn't for me.

"My dad was more corporate. He couldn't understand why I'd want to step away from that world. He was on the cover of BusinessWeek. *But that was never my goal, and I couldn't care less – I like to have impact with real people.*

"As a woman, I'm aware of how many women still feel intimidated about financial issues. I wanted to empower my clients to feel there's no such thing as a stupid question. It's their money, they can ask what they want. I'm now on my second generation of clients. And I love having that ability to help other families – because let's face it, we parents aren't going to be around forever.

"I wanted to work part-time because of the flexibility it gave me – I had a young family, I wanted to be there more for them. I want to help other families have what I had.

"My biggest passion is educating people who may not have had access before. I feel like the entire financial services industry has underserved women and younger people. I want to change that. My company is a major disruptor – we use an all-digital platform, and can educate people about the value of life insurance and fundamental investment strategies, programs with low minimums, or no minimums."

The Consultant Community.

Are these your people? Do you want to hang out with them, or do you feel like you were just kidnapped and sucked up into a UFO? Do you relate to, and trust, the person introducing you to the company and the people they introduce you to? If you join the business, they're likely to be in your orbit on the regular, either online, in person, or both. It's important to get a gut check: Do they have an energy that elevates you? Do you feel they care about you? Ask yourself, can I see myself here?

Pepz Javier found his fit in a Foreign Exchange trading and education company with a community he loved.

"I was with a lifestyle brand Network Marketing company when I first graduated from college. I wasn't crazy about the products, but I loved the culture – it opened my mind to the value of personal growth. And I had a great group of friends from that company!

"I never imagined I'd end up doing something in finance. I'm an artist – music, dance, and acting are my passion. During the 2020 Covid crisis, a lot of my income dried up. I had an inkling that I should revisit Network Marketing, so I reached out to a few of my friends from my old company.

"I heard they were with my new company, learning how to trade on the foreign exchange market themselves, and using the Network Marketing arm of the company to create revenue from referrals. And they were having significant success. Even though I'd never even heard of the foreign exchange market, I jumped at the chance to work with them, learn how to trade, and show other people how to do that, too! And it's been fantastic!"

And of Course: The Money, Honey.

Look at their compensation plan. Is it simple or complicated? You want someone to be able to explain the basics in a few sentences, and the nuances without having to go back to calculus class.

What's the average that people are making at each level? How long does it take on average to start making that? Do they pay weekly or monthly (or, like my company, both)? For some people, this timing will matter less; for others, weekly commission payouts can be a lifeline.

Just as importantly, what will it take out-of-pocket to "get into the game?" It takes money to make money, as they say – but how much? If there's a suggested buy-in for products, what is it? And, if you apply yourself, how fast can you earn that back and start to be in profit? Some people are longer time-horizon people – others prefer to go with a company where you can potentially earn back your investment within the first 90 days. Find a company whose pay plan matches your desires and goals.

Some people have a single issue "aha" moment. For others, it's the confluence of factors that makes a particular company feel right.

Dina Michael and her husband Elan found their fit with an Insurance and investment company that matched both their missions and their financial desires.

Dina says: *"My grandmother taught me to appreciate investments, and want to have a big nest egg. I started my career doing post-production work for a TV company. It wasn't a dream job, but I thought it could be a path to success. And I had a mentor there who I thought was really successful because he had all the trappings of "the good life" – gorgeous home, fancy cars, all that stuff. Then I found out he was actually in huge debt, and struggling emotionally because of it.*

"That was a light bulb moment for me. After seeing his stress, I vowed to ALWAYS have savings, a retirement plan, and financial peace of mind. So I decided to get myself a financial advisor! And during my research, I was referred to my Network Marketing company.

"I didn't see myself in this industry initially; however, the more I thought about it, the more I felt drawn to it. I realized that financial literacy- especially for women – is what's important to me. And the more people I met here, the more at home I felt. My colleagues became like family.

"I love teaching people how money works. And I love helping people. Our company is a great place to do both."

Elan says: *"In my twenties, I was working in a restaurant. There was an older gentleman who came in every week with his wife, and they seemed to have a very comfortable, relaxed lifestyle. And one day the man said to me, "And what do you want to do for your future? If you were to work in my industry you would earn more in a month than you do now in a year." I said, "Tell me more!" He said, "I'm in the insurance business."*

"*So, I became an insurance agent at his company! And I really liked it! But he was still the owner... I was just an employee. Then a friend invited me to an event with my current company, where I learned I could build and own my OWN business. This made total sense to me.*

"*I love helping families plan for their futures. My own included – I met my wife because we both had our own businesses here. And now we have four kids!*"

All this might seem like a fair amount to assess, but it doesn't need to take a lot of time. You can often discover what you need to know during the first meeting or introduction to a company – in fact most Network Marketing companies aim to offer you all the info you need to make a decision right away. Learn from my mistake of spending four months in drill down mode, and don't overthink it. But do pay attention to your gut feelings. If you have questions, make sure you get to someone with answers that satisfy you.

Finding your fit is so PERSONAL that even having the same DNA doesn't mean you'll end up at the same Network Marketing Company. Check out these "Twins With Different Wins:"

Twin 1 is Samantha Wright, who's doing very well with a Network Marketing company specializing in essential oils. Twin 2, Michelle McGregor, is a Yale Drama School graduate who's doing very well with our company.

Samantha says: "*One day I was casually messaging a doula colleague of mine about life and work when she mentioned that she'd recently retired her husband thanks to her essential oils business.*

"I was speechless. I didn't even know she had another business! I'd just seen her sharing a bit about essential oils on social media from time to time. I had to learn more.

"We went out for coffee and she shared with me about the company and about how these products were really helping people and families take back their health. I thought, this is crazy! I've been sharing about natural wellness options with others my entire life, but I never knew I could get paid for it!

"I dove in fast. I learned all I could about this new-to-me concept of "Network Marketing," and I experienced my company's products firsthand. They really worked! Sharing about them was effortless and fun for me. I felt at home with the community of teammates I was getting to know, and I was earning enough income my first month to really make a difference for my family.

"I felt like I was home. I love working for a company that lives to serve others through health and wellness, and that prioritizes quality, integrity, and sustainability."

Michelle says: "When a divorce turned my financial life turned upside down, I knew that the money I was making as a performer was not enough (at least not yet) to continue living in Los Angeles. Taking up a job waiting tables again was going to interfere far too much with the 12-16 hours of work I was already doing daily as an artist: driving around town for auditions, nightly rehearsals for a play, and late evening practices and gigs with my bands. No way was I going to sacrifice half of my pursuits and priorities to some waitressing gig. That's when I turned to my twin sister and said, "I want to do this oils business with *you." I thought I did. I didn't know exactly what that would look like, but I knew she was making good money building a business with her company.*

"Then I went to her company's convention. I had a great time being there with her — but I realized while I was there that the products just weren't really my jam. And when the training started, it just. Didn't. Land.

"I went to a meeting of my current company (we'll call it company B) simply to see if I could learn something from these B people that I could apply towards my sister's company. And that's when I learned just how different Network Marketing companies can be from one another.

"And in company B there were so many other actors, singers, producers, many of whom were very successful in their creative careers. I was impressed to learn that a Broadway actress, a multi-platinum songwriter, a famous talk show host, and a crazy successful Canadian singer were all building businesses with company B. And the products, the comp plan, the method they used to spread the word, all just clicked for me.

"My sister's company is kicking ass. But her business just wasn't for me. And you know what? That's why Baskin Robbins has 31 flavors."

As these stories show, there is a Network Marketing company for just about everyone. **The bottom line is, when it's right, you know it.** The risk is small. Just jump in and try the products, meet the people, and if you like the vibe, join the tribe.

Chapter 8

Use the Blueprint to Build

YAY! You've found your fit – a strong company with just your kind of people, products, and philosophy. And you've decided to say YES. CONGRATS! Obviously, your first job is to be a regular user of whatever your company offers. I mean, would you trust a Tesla dealer who drove a Chevy? And if you're going to Ivy up, here's what's next.

 Master and Duplicate the 8-Step Blueprint to Build.

The Blueprint is a series of learnable, teachable actions designed to connect you to enough people who might be looking for what you have, and share enough information so that they can decide to refer others, buy products, or join you in the business. If they decide to join you, the Blueprint will help them learn to duplicate these same actions themselves.

Clearly, the ultimate goal of the Blueprint is sales. While in Real Estate the magic words are "location, location, location," in Network Marketing, they're "duplication, duplication, duplication."

First follow the Blueprint. Then duplicate yourself by teaching the Blueprint to other people on your team, who will then learn and duplicate it as well. And so on, and so on, and so on.

And hey, eight steps might sound like a lot. It's possible in this social-media heavy age to say that all you need to duplicate is "share, sell, sign up, repeat" – or, if you are with a party-based company, "post, host, sign up, repeat." While these are essential, they're not the whole story.

The whole story is the whole Blueprint, the gold standard, Ivy League plan for duplication, because it addresses both what needs to happen between your ears as well as between you and your clients and teammates.

Happily, the Blueprint is what I call NRS – Not Rocket Science. I know this with 100% certainty because we have an actual rocket scientist on our team, Caitlin O'Connell. She says, "Following the Blueprint is not rocket science." NRS is why we don't have to reinvent the wheel, even as we are reinventing ourselves.

However, the Blueprint isn't child's play, either. Every step requires time, effort, and skill.

The steps to the Blueprint are:

Identify, Invite, Share, Follow Up, Sign Up, Launch, Plug In, Repeat.

IDENTIFY people who might be interested in your products or business.

INVITE them to take a look at what you have to offer.

SHARE emotionally impactful information.

FOLLOW UP with them.

SIGN UP new clients or business partners.

LAUNCH new business partners.

PLUG IN to events, training, and personal growth.

REPEAT.

Let's get under the hood of each of these a bit.

1. IDENTIFY

The first step is to identify all the people you're connected to and can ask to take a look at what you have to offer – in biz terminology, "prospects." Happily, most of us will find a large number of prospects just by turning on our phones or glancing at our social media. Put your prospects on a list. Include everyone – without prejudging who you think will and won't be interested in what you have to offer.

In the industry, this is known as your "100 PERSON LIST," though there is nothing sacred about the number 100. It's basically a data dump of the people you currently know – or used to know but can still find. From your list, choose the five to ten prospects who you would be most excited to have as business partners: the smartest, most successful, most influential, most fun, most get-it-done humans you know. They will be your business Dream Team.

Then choose five to ten prospects you believe will be most eager to hear about the product side of your business – your Dream Clients. Your Dream Team and your Dream Clients will be the first prospects you approach.

Oh, and do yourself one quick favor. In this business, you choose who your client and business partner base will be. So, if you know someone and really don't like them, cross them off your list.

Your list will be a key aspect of your business, ongoing. Make it, and then continually, deliberately expand it – identifying and adding new prospects whom you meet (in person or online), or to whom you are referred.

2. INVITE.

Having prospects is of no use at all unless you take action by authentically connecting and inviting them to check out what you've got. So, whether you're texting, emailing, connecting through DM, IM or even calling someone (remember that?), authentically connect by showing you give a hoot about who they are and how they're doing. And if you think it would feel random to them that you're reaching out, say so.

Then, right away, stay authentic by explaining that you're reaching out for a business reason. Because in this day and age, while everyone's looking for connection, we also have our BS meters set to high alert. So don't bait with friendship and switch to business later – just put it out there right away. That way, you have personally connected in a business context.

Next, tell them why you thought of them. Be complimentary, and again, authentic.

Also, be honest about what you don't know. As in, "I have no idea whether this would be a fit for you." Because you DON'T know… yet.

Now, invite them to check out what you're up to. Keep it light. And never insist. Permission is key. One way to get permission is to simply ask, "Are you open?" As in, "Are you open to taking a look at this?" or "Are you open to trying this out?" or "Are you open to a short chat?"

Alternatively, Eric Worre's magic phrase, "If I …would you…" works like a charm. It's respectful, not demanding. If someone says yes, you have agreement. And if they say no, no big deal.

"If I sent you an overview, would you check it out?" *Just wondering.*

"If I shared a quick video, would you take a look?" *I'm interested in knowing.*

"If I invited you onto a short Zoom, would you come?" *It's your choice.*

"If I had time Friday afternoon to explain it, would you be free?" *The ball is in your court.*

Here are examples of how it can sound when you put it all together:

"Hi Max, how are you? I'm reaching out because I've actually started a business. I'm looking for a few amazing people to partner with, and you're one of the most ambitious humans I know. I have no idea

whether this would be a fit for you, but if I sent you a link to an overview, would you check it out?"

"Hello, Ja'Nice, hope all's good on your end. I've started a new business. I know you're into looking good and I think you'd love the products. I'm having a little online event Sunday at 7:00 to kick things off. Are you open to jumping on?"

"Hi Jason — long time no see. I actually have a business thing to run by you, but I'd love to know how you are ...tell me what's up in your world. I've started a side hustle I think might be up your alley as a busy dad. If I invited you to a short Zoom, would you check it out?"

"Hey, Crystal, hope you're well. I know this is totally random, but I can see from your posts that you have a genuine love of health and fitness. I don't know if you're familiar with what I do, but after seeing some of your posts, I feel like you would absolutely rock at it. Have you ever considered creating a business alongside what you're already doing? It's totally cool either way, but are you open to learning a bit more?"

Will you always get a yes? NO. And that's actually ok. *It's a relief when people are open about being closed.* Your time is valuable and so is theirs. But most people will say **yes** to at least looking at, hearing about, or learning about something new. And because they've given you **permission,** there's **no doubt** in either of your minds about what's happening, and **no weirdness** about getting them the info.

3. SHARE EMOTIONALLY IMPACTFUL INFORMATION.

Once your prospect has said yes to your invitation, it's time to share. Your company will have tools – e.g. a website, videos, online meetings, or events – already templated for you. Through these, you will share information about both the company, its products, and the business.

But your prospect doesn't just need information. They need inspiration. 'Cuz the fact about facts is, they're not really driving our decisions. Emotions are. Your prospect's bottom-line questions are always emotion driven: will what you are offering make me feel better – or not feel so bad – about something in my life? In other words, they will always be thinking, **"What's so great about that?"** and **"Why should I care?"**

If your company's tools are good, they will have emotionally impactful information built in. If your company's tools are less emotionally moving, be sure to point out to your prospect what IS so great about what you have, and why they SHOULD care.

And here's a crazy thing: no matter what you share in terms of both information and inspiration, the most important thing you share is YOU. **You,** with **your** energy, telling **your** story, may be enough to have someone say "I'm in." We often say that people don't join a company, they join YOU. And it's true.

4. FOLLOW UP.

"The fortune is in the follow up," so now that you've shared your business and your products, it's time to see what your prospect wants to do.

The point of a follow up is to get to a **YES**, a **NO**, a **NO FOR NOW,** or a **NEXT APPOINTMENT**. I know, you might have thought it's always *to get to a YES*. If Network Marketers were in the convincing business, that might be true. But we're in the sorting business – sorting through the people on our list to see who wants what we've got. Some will, some won't. Some now, some later. Some as consumers, some as team members.

The keys to a successful follow up are: asking questions, handling objections, confidently recommending, and either sealing the deal or setting the next appointment.

I love the follow up method I learned. It begins with just two questions. The first is, "So, what interested you most about what you heard (or saw or read)?" BAM. You don't have to be a mind reader. They just tell you what they care about – whether that's something on the product end, what your company stands for, or the financial opportunity. Whatever my prospect says to this first question, I always say, "Great!" Because it is.

My second question is always, "On a scale of 1-10." You want to know your prospect's current truth fast, whether they are hot, lukewarm, or cold *about the business*. Even if their first exposure is to a product-centric tool, because you're in a Network Marketing company, there will be at least a mention of the fact that there's a business opportunity attached to these products. And that's what you want to know about first.

I look to keep it casual: "So, about the business part of this. On a scale of 1-10, with ten being "this business sounds brilliant! Sign me up!" and one being "I would rather stick pins in my eyes," where do you see yourself?" If someone is a ten, they're a YES! Woo-hoo! Enrolling business partners is step one in duplicating yourself.

If someone is a five through nine, they're a maybe. Your job is to address any of those pesky **yeah, buts**.

If they're an eight or a nine, they're close to a yes. You want to find out what would get them to yes. This is NRS – *"Sounds like you're really close to jumping in. What would get you to a ten right now?"*

If they're a six or seven, they're leaning positive, but have some hesitations. You want to discover what they are, and offer assistance. *"Sounds like you might have some questions. Perhaps I can shed some light."*

If they're a five, they are neither here nor there. You want to find out why, and help them move to one side or the other. *"Sounds like you're really on the fence. Tell me what's on your mind."*

If they're under a five, they're a NO for the business… or at least a NO FOR NOW. You want to stop talking business. *"Totally cool – this business isn't for everyone. Let's just talk about the products."*

I'll come back to the products in a minute. Let's stay on your 5-9s, who will likely bring up one or more of the common *yeah, buts* found in Chapter 6. Remember, objections aren't necessarily rejections. You want to handle objections, not shy away from them.

First, acknowledge the objection. Say it's the time objection. You can say, "I totally hear you. A lot of people feel they don't have time to add a new business into their busy lives. I even felt that way myself."

Then educate your prospect, "What I found was that this can actually be done really effectively in small bits of time, if someone is motivated. A text here, a call there, having people watch something themselves while you're doing something else … it can really add up." You can end with another question, "Make sense?"

LISTEN to their responses, and if there are further questions, answer them, too.

Then, confidently recommend they join you, and see if they're ready to take action. If they are, GREAT! If they're not, connect them to any information you think will help them decide what's right for them, and set a next appointment, preferably within a day or two.

At the next appointment, keep the process going. Ask questions. Handle objections. Confidently recommend they join you in the business and see if they are ready. Repeat as necessary.

They will either say yes to the business or no to the business. If they say no, say, "That's totally fine. This business isn't for everyone. Let's just talk about the products."

OK, now that you have worked through the follow up for enrolling someone onto your team, let's talk follow up for product sales.

The 1-10 scale works just as well to gauge your prospect's interest about products. Using my own company as an example, a ten might be, "Yes! I want to switch to a clean, safe brand right now!" and one is, "Nah, I'm good with my toxic products." Or, for our signature nutrition program, ten might be, "Wow! This reboot is exactly what I've been looking for!" And one is, "Heck no – I am 100% happy with how I look and feel."

Based on their interest, make a recommendation. Recommend things HIGHLY and with true enthusiasm. For example, I say: "I *highly* recommend that you become what we call a Preferred Client. It's a program where you can get 20-40% off all your purchases for a year, plus free shipping and a free product of your choice with every qualifying order. Would you like to do this?" If they are a YES for the products, great.

And if they are a NO for the products, it's fine.

If someone is a NO for both business and products, let them know it's *totally ok* if this isn't right for them. However, **ALWAYS** ask for referrals for the products *and* for the business. It's done in every other type of business – why not this one? Referrals are often the best candidates for **anything**! Again, NRS. Like this: "I totally understand if this isn't a fit for you in any way. However, I'm wondering if you're open to giving me a few referrals, because I believe you'll know at least a couple of people who are looking for what we have."

My suggestion, from painful experience, is that you look to get referrals on the spot. It can be as easy as, "Who pops into your head?" (And then stop talking.) When you put it this way, your prospect will often actually have a couple of people pop into their head. Then, ask them to connect you, right then and there, on a 3-way DM, text, or email. Let them know that all they need to do is introduce you, not try to explain your business or products at all. You can even offer to write something for them to just copy and paste.

If there's no one popping into their head, schedule a time to check back with them in the next day or two to see who's come to mind. And let them know how grateful you are, in advance, for their referrals.

However, sometimes your prospect will say the dreaded words, "I'll let you know if I think of someone." Usually this is code for, "I will never refer you to anyone." Move on. Plenty of fish in the sea.

Lastly, even if someone is a NO for the business, the products, and for referrals, always ask permission to touch base again in the future. Things can change. Maybe they will, and maybe they won't. So, when you ask if it's ok to check back in the future, it's not that you are distrusting or disrespecting someone's NO. It's just that NO may or may not be a NO FOR NOW and neither you nor your prospect know that until later. Life happens. And when life happens, people sometimes make new choices. Sometimes about products, sometimes about business. In fact, lots of now satisfied clients, and many of the most successful Network Marketers, were definite, absolute NOs the first (and maybe the second, third and sixth) time they were asked.

Now let's get to the good stuff: what to do with a YES.

5. SIGN UP.

Whether it's for products or to be a business partner, as soon as your prospect says yes, SIGN THEM UP.

When someone wants products, BE EXCITED FOR THEM. VALIDATE THEIR CHOICE. Help them enroll as a consumer, place their first order, and learn how to get the best deals. You want as many clients as possible, happily ordering as often as possible.

If someone wants to join your business team, BE EXCITED FOR THEM. VALIDATE THEIR CHOICE. Help them enroll as a business partner, place their first order, and get the best deals. If possible, show your newbie exactly how you do the sign up, because part of their job will be to do the same thing. And then move right along to the next step:

6. LAUNCH.

Launching means helping your new partner start their business right. You will lead them through a few processes that give them the best chance to succeed by being in the right mindset, having the right expectations, and taking the right actions to begin to see results ASAP.

Every company has their own launch rituals, but they all involve welcoming your newbie to the team, helping them clarify why they said yes, explaining how your mentorship will work, connecting them to your company's resources, and "opening for business" through time-leveraging activities. Here's how to Ivy League your launching a newbie.

Introduce Them to the Team, and the Team to Them.

In Network Marketing, you're in business *for* yourself but not *by* yourself. Community counts, and you are your newbie's portal to their new pool of mentors and fellow teammates. Celebrate what's best about your newbie in your team intro so they can feel known and appreciated right off the bat. And personally help them follow or connect them to anyone who you think they will relate to or enjoy.

Get Agreement on the Basics.

Ask your newbie WHY they're doing the business. Find out what they're looking to get from it, how much time they estimate they'll have each week, and for how long they'll agree to put in the effort required to see their work pay off. Let them know that, as their partner, you will support them in their business and meet their effort every step of the way. And that you expect them to show you _by their actions_ that they deserve your time.

Set Reasonable Goals.

Help your newbie choose an attainable first goal – your company will let you know the choices. Spell out what that will get them in terms of dollars or a promotion. Let your newbie know it's work, but that it's doable if they are coachable and committed.

Be Their Guide.

Show your newbie how and where to find info on the business and products. You, as their partner, will advise them on how to reach out to prospects. And you'll take the lead in their first events, presentations, and follow up conversations so that your newbie can see and hear what you do and begin learning how to duplicate it themselves.

Treat Them Like a Grownup.

Instead of taking your time over and over to do things *for* your newbie, show them – once – where to find the info to learn how to do things for themselves. No spoon-feeding. It's like you're saying, "You bought yourself a car. Congrats! It's a great vehicle. I'm here to help you learn how to drive it. My job is to show you how to be an independent driver as soon as possible, so you can show others how to drive their own cars, too. I can't drive it *for* you; however, I can show you where the gas pedal, brake, steering wheel, and seatbelts are, tell you the rules of the road, and refer you to our excellent online school. In the beginning, while you practice, I can be in the car with you on a dual brake system as you get the hang of it. Then, you will control your own speed and determine your own destination."

7. PLUG IN.

Executing the Blueprint takes effort, and effort requires energy. Because you can't simply keep driving forever with no gas in the tank (or electricity in the battery), you'll need to "plug in and refuel" on a regular basis. Your mentors will guide you to helpful meetings, trainings, conferences, books, videos, audios, and team conversations, both large and small. You'll regularly reconnect with your community, and you'll become more skilled and more confident.

Plugging in is non-negotiable for Ivy Leaguers. When you need the latest info, plug in. When your belief, or your energy, or your enthusiasm for your business is flagging, plug in. Oh, and when you're excited, plug in so that others can get a little of what you have.

When YOU plug in, and show others how to plug in, you grow, they grow, and so does your business. And their business. And so on, and so on, and so on.

8. REPEAT.

You can't do these steps once and expect to build a business. Network Marketing is iterative. You'll need to do these steps again and again and again.

The Blueprint is tried and true. Each step is critical. And the more often and attentively you do each step, the more efficient you will become at building your business the Ivy League Way. Therefore:

 Make the Dean's List in Duplication.

Duplication is the key to sanity and profit, because duplication is key to leveraging your time. Leveraging your time leverages your impact, and allows you to serve the most additional people with the least additional effort. Do not distract yourself by trying to "do business a better way." Duplicate the Blueprint.

And remember, online and off, at every stage of the Blueprint, what you do duplicates. All the good stuff, and all the other stuff too. So, if you're talking to someone, one-on-one, for hours, **before** they decide to join you, you're showing them that this business takes a lot of time. If they join you, they'll duplicate that. However, if you're sending them a quick DM, and then inviting them to a short group event, and then doing a quick follow up, you're showing them that this business can be done quickly. If they join, they'll duplicate that. So:

🍃 *Duplicate the Blueprint, but Don't Just Duplicate the Blueprint.*

That's nuts and bolts for good performance, "necessary but not sufficient" as they say in legalese. To be truly Ivy, duplicate the sensibilities of the highest achievers. Duplicate COMMITMENT. Duplicate GENEROSITY. Duplicate PASSION. Duplicate FIRE! Duplicate FUN!

Chapter 9

If at First You Don't Succeed

So, you've found your Network Marketing fit, and there's a Blueprint to Build. Learn it, execute it and get results. Pretty straightforward. Phew! But if everyone succeeded just because there was a way to do it, quickly becoming a Network Marketing success story would be a guarantee. Newsflash, it's not.

Take me, for example. Did I make the Dean's List in Duplication? More like the Dean's List in Complication. In fact, I **sucked** when I started my business. I'll tell you about it, just in case you've started your business and feel like you suck, too.

Actually, in my overachieving way, when I started my business, I didn't *just* suck. I *sucked-so-bad*. Why? Well, to avoid stressing myself, I didn't actually hold myself accountable to the Blueprint. I wanted success, but I wasn't truly committed to it.

I justified this by the fact that, as I mentioned earlier, I was physically ill with this mysterious, but very real and debilitating, condition. Above the neck I spent my days in "cog fog" – I had trouble thinking straight or keeping focused, and often words weren't there when I went to find them. Below the neck, I never knew when I'd have enough energy to do things, or when I'd end up lying in bed so paralyzed by exhaustion that I literally couldn't pull the blanket up.

But looking back, to be honest, even if I had been full of chirpy cheerleader energy every moment of every day, I would still have *sucked-so-bad* because I had another paralyzing illness, and this one was purely mental: **fear**.

Not just fear in its oft-quoted meaning of FALSE EVIDENCE APPEARING REAL, though that was definitely true. In my case fear stood for "FREAKED OUT, EMBARRASSED, ANXIOUS, and RESISTANT."

I was **FREAKED OUT** that I might be perceived as a salesperson, which at the time I thought was a bad thing. I had the mistaken belief that people who sell were doing something **to** other people – I didn't yet get they could be doing something **for** other people. I thought of myself solely as a *businessperson* – in the business of offering people a business of their own. When I did work up the courage to talk to someone and they weren't interested in joining my business, I didn't talk to them about simply being a product user. Yeesh! Can you imagine – all those people still using toxic products – plus all that money left on the table.

EMBARRASSED – boy, was I. *Even though I knew* that Network Marketing was a bulletproof business model. *Even though I knew* that all savvy, successful people have multiple streams of income, and *even though I knew* that actually, the new economics of the music business had failed me (and so many others), there was a part of me that worried that people might think I had – gasp – failed in music and "had to" do this. So I remained in the closet with my entire professional music circle, who comprised about half my list.

Next, I was truly, madly, deeply **ANXIOUS** about speaking in public – or on camera. Can you relate, or rather, commiserate? Since that fateful day during my fifth grade school musical when, to my horror, I forgot an entire verse of my solo song, the idea of *eyes on me* left me terrified. As soon as I tried to talk at a presentation, I became a red-faced, brain-drained, fretting, forgetting, sweating ball of fugly.

Lastly, my signature impatience made me totally **RESISTANT** to following a Blueprint. I'm an Aries – a new/now/next kinda person. Step-by-step is not my style. I don't read the manuals for my electronics, and I go cross-eyed at recipes. I just want what I want *right away*. Thus, even though part of me was screaming, "Would someone please tell me what to do?" another part was screaming even louder, "Don't tell me what to do!" Know what I mean?

Given all of this, it was no surprise that I had an epic fail at one of the Blueprint's main steps for newbies: launching.

In our company, at the time, the recommendation was to have four launches. But I only worked up the nerve to have one launch, and it was a disaster. I was too FREAKED OUT at the thought of asking a lot of people. Too EMBARRASSED to "sell" the concept of changing your brand, much less potentially changing your life. Too ANXIOUS to speak with any impact. And too RESISTANT to correctly follow the steps for the event – starting with getting my mentor on video with us, since she was 3000 miles away.

No surprise, then, when after my lone launch, *no one* purchased anything, *no one* joined my team, and *no one* referred me to anyone. Or that I used *that* failure to justify why I wouldn't do another launch. Bush league, not Ivy League.

And it didn't get much better during those first few months. In fact, I got really defensive. When I did talk to someone, I alternated between shy (beating around the bush), verbose ("So...lemmetellyafiftyreasonswhythisissogreat"), and strident ("What's your *problem*? Don't you see that this is genius?") Afterwards, I didn't follow up correctly, because I was afraid of rejection. What a waste.

So, if you are reading this and happened to be among the first oh, say, 300 people I spoke to after starting my business, **I'M SORRY!** I very likely either vomited information, was indirect, or insufferable. Maybe I was too self-conscious to tell you what might be possible for you or the people you care about, or too insistent that I really did have the answer for your life. Perhaps I was annoying or timid or went on and on endlessly without checking to see if you were actually interested – or whatever. In other words, I made it about me and not you. **I'd love to have a do-over.** Please write and let me know if you're up for it. My email is: amyyousuckedsobad@ivyleaguenetworkmarketing.com.

But even though I *sucked-so-bad,* I am actually grateful for it now, because in case this is even a little bit you, I get to be your living proof that you can start, *suck-so-bad,* and still make it to the top.

Here are the first Ivy League tips I employed to turn my bush league, fear-based failure around.

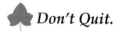 ## Don't Quit.

I mean, why start a business just to stop it?

My first check was… ready? $45.84. Barely enough to take my family to the movies. I could have looked at that as proof that this currently traumatic side hustle wasn't worth it. But I didn't, because I had heard from my super successful upline Sue Cassidy that her first check was *$8.71!* Mostly anyone would look at an $8.71 check and say, "See? This doesn't work!" Sue, however, saw it as proof that this DID work, that *actual* money came from her effort, and that this could be the beginning of something HUGE. And she was right. As I mentioned before, she now has the largest international business in the company.

However, truth be told, even if I'd never known Sue personally, or her story, quitting was not on my menu. Anyone who leaves a new endeavor when they're not an overnight success really only had "one foot in" in the first place.

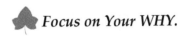 *Focus on Your WHY.*

Whenever I had a tough moment – radio silence, nasty text, whatever – I reminded myself WHY I'd started in the first place: to feel relieved, not panicked, when I looked at my bank balance. I'd ask myself questions like, "If not this, what's my plan B? Do I *really* want to simply cross my fingers and hope the music business will magically recover? Do I *really* want to go back to school and pay to retrain for something new that won't guarantee a job? Do I *really* want to turn my future over to other people who could decide I was too old or too sick, too overqualified, or too underqualified, or that they didn't like my look or my religion or my gender? Do I *really* want to try to find a full-time job, with my exhaustion so pronounced, and the kids' childhoods slipping away ever more quickly? Do I *really* want to live smaller and give up my dreams of a better life?" No, no, no, no, and no. **THAT'S WHY.**

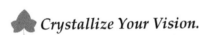 *Crystallize Your Vision.*

I imagined what life would look like when I'd achieved my WHY. I allowed myself to actually write it out, a verbal picture of my "someday" personal world, filled with all the ease and abundance that I didn't have at the moment. Then I got woo-woo and made a vision board that I would look at daily. Mine had pictures of all the things that represented ease and abundance to me: calm people doing yoga, Hawaiian plumeria, diamonds, dolphins, pristine beaches, happy pictures of my family. It also had pictures of money – the money I'd have for our kids' college, for our retirement, and for charity. Money in stacks, money hiding in the grass, and money literally growing on trees. Collaged on top were positive words and phrases snipped from magazines: "soaring vision," "peace of mind," "lead from the heart," "WOW… a team as ambitious as your goals," "put the power of a network of 5,000 to work for you," and "REPEAT."

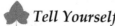 *Tell Yourself a Different Story.*

I knew I needed to seriously shift who I thought I was. Because if my current situation was the story of my life, it did not feel like a page-turner. So, I made it a habit to describe what I wanted to happen, as if it had already happened, and feel, somehow, as if it were true… just for a moment. When I couldn't feel like it was true, I said it again and again until it at least felt a little less false.

For example, even when I still couldn't lead *myself* out of a paper bag, I forced myself to look in the bathroom mirror and say, "I am a leader of leaders." I remember literally crying the first time I did this, because it felt so BS. But I did it, and did it, until it started to seem just a tiny bit more legit.

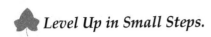 *Level Up in Small Steps.*

For example, my personal style. When I started with my company, I was a busy mom who wrote songs from home. No one cared how I looked when I went to the grocery store or the gym. I wore schleppy sweatpants, didn't use makeup, and did my nails myself – about as well as any Kindergartener. Now that I was a brand ambassador, recommending a major brand and business, I thought to myself, *If I met me, would I listen to me about… anything?* NO! So I decided to invest in one or two decent outfits (and YES, on killer sale, I don't believe in retail), learned the art of our "five-minute face" using my company's makeup, and found a manicurist. Not only did people start to take me more seriously – I took myself more seriously.

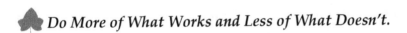 *Do More of What Works and Less of What Doesn't.*

Kicking and screaming inside, I looked honestly at what wasn't working and vowed to do a little less wrong and a little more right. I began following the Blueprint on a semi-regular basis. Because I was still often sick, I allowed myself to reschedule dates if I was exhausted, even dates with myself. I needed to go a bit more slowly at times.

I stopped vomiting information, or literally begging people to listen. I started talking to a few more people every week. I stopped taking "no" quite so personally. I watched a couple more trainings. I took a few more of my mentor's suggestions.

I started getting educated on how to build and run a team. I started approaching a few people in my primary profession. I got a little better at inviting people to become consumers if they weren't into joining the business.

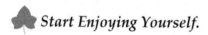 *Start Enjoying Yourself.*

I realized that I'd been thinking about doing the work as if it were a slog. So, duh, I stopped. I began actually looking forward to learning more and doing more of this business, and to the self-growth and self-care that came with it. I reminded myself that life could be FUN, that I wasn't the only one looking for that, and that I could lead by example.

And wonder of wonders, when I did all these things, a few people actually purchased products, and a few other people actually joined my business. I still sorta *sucked*, but I didn't *suck-so-bad.* I'd learned that when you commit to using the Blueprint, out yourself as a professional Network Marketer, and start trusting in the process and in your abilities, the Blueprint starts to work in your favor. And you start to make progress, and money, too – yah freakin' hoo. I mean, who doesn't want more money? In my case, my checks started being more like $458.40 than $45.84. Not earth-shattering, but headed in the right direction. Plus, at this point I had enough sales volume to achieve my first promotion in our four level compensation plan.

Clearly, my business didn't have a pretty beginning. And you know what? So what? Perhaps the most important tip I can offer from my first months in Network Marketing is:

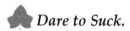 *Dare to Suck.*

Stumbling is humbling, but it's what needs to happen before you get decent, which is what needs to happen before you get good. Plus, it's important for potential and current teammates to see that they don't have to be experts in order to do this kind of a business. Anyone can stumble forward. Companies actually anticipate that newbies will need practice. In our company, for instance, we have a cheat sheet of notes for our presentations, which I have seen many people simply use verbatim until they feel familiar enough to go "off book." It communicates, and you don't have to worry that you'll leave out something important. But it proves a point, too. You don't have to be great. All you need to do to get going is read, smile, and be yourself. And remember, you won't suck forever. Practice makes better.

Now look – I hope you never have any of my fears, and never *suck-so-bad*. But if you do, it's ok. You won't die. I didn't. In fact, I was just getting started. And maybe you are too.

Chapter 10

People, Purpose, and Passion Are Required, Not Optional

Have you learned from my rookie mistakes? I hope so. Are you ready to achieve more? Great. I've learned that "ready" often comes in stages. Here's what mine were, and the Ivy League Tips I learned at each.

After my first promotion, I was ready to give myself a little tough love. What had to change for me to go further? I realized that I needed to get my "ask" in gear and invite WAY more prospects. And that I'd been resisting ramping up my "asks" because of my lingering discomfort around appearing salesy, and around rejection.

So I bit the bullet and began to employ the **"You know what? So what?"** method. As in, "Okay, people might think I'm salesy, but you know what? So what?" or "Okay, I'll get turned down by a bunch of people. You know what? So what?"

I started to lock myself in my office with my maltipoo Sadie, reminding us both before each "ask" that *people are looking for what we have.* She never disagreed.

Not everyone was looking, and some of the ones who weren't were pretty rude. But enough people WERE looking. A few more on the business side (helped by my authentically sharing that I was having a bit of success in that department). And a number more on the client side, helped by my personal face care results. My glow was undeniable, which made it easier for "all business" me to pivot to enthusiastic product recommender.

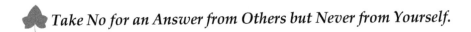 *Take No for an Answer from Others but Never from Yourself.*

Stop stopping yourself from your full potential. Whatever's restricting your growth, you can't afford – literally or metaphorically – to let it rule you.

After about a year of following the Blueprint (not perfectly, but well ENOUGH) and doing the do part-time, I promoted to the second of our four levels of achievement. There, I started earning checks with commas in them, and that felt GOOD. Plus, I felt more relaxed overall, because at this level in our company, your business becomes a willable asset.

That was huge for me. When the economy and music business tanked, I had felt so disheartened about not pulling my financial weight in the family. Now, not only was I starting to, but if something happened to me, my husband (or whoever I designated, so he'd better keep being nice to me) could step in and receive my checks, or even *grow* the business. What a relief!

I got to this level in the average time for our company, which kinda irked me, actually, because I wasn't used to being average. (I know – cue world's smallest violin.)

But getting there upped my belief in myself, in our brand, in the Blueprint, and in the model of Network Marketing. And if you have chosen Network Marketing, with whatever company, it's likely that if you stick with it long enough, you'll turn a similar financial and emotional corner.

 ## *Course Correct and Keep Going.*

Fix what needs fixing and continue on your journey no matter what. Positive shifts *will* come if you are willing to stay the course and put in the effort.

At this stage, I realized that I wanted more local support. I said to Linda, "There must be *someone* cool in LA who is doing this business." She told me about some chick named Claire Risoli, and said she thought we'd hit it off.

I couldn't have Claire over fast enough. She was a fierce, fun Latinx actor and mom, with a serious marketing background to boot, and the same "in it to win it" attitude as me. We instantly made a vow to join forces and support each other to the top.

 ## *Find A Running Buddy.*

Solo is a no-no in this business. Yes, we're all solo in that we own our own businesses, but it can be exhausting to feel like we're out there on our own all the time. Business is better with a buddy, whether you're urging each other on, catching each other when you fall, or even engaging in a little playful competition.

What started out as a one-on-one at my breakfast room table blossomed into a think tank of abundance-minded self-starters. Claire and I gathered a posse of like-minded "sideline" business partners who – though we didn't benefit from one another at all financially – locked arms to share our learning, our homes, our voices, and our visions.

We dubbed our crew "LA Connect." We got into a groove, had meetings for ourselves and our prospects, gave and took helpful advice, picked each other up after no- shows or unexpected setbacks, and found the fun big time.

And when our homes wouldn't hold us all, we started renting out spaces in hotels, restaurants, libraries, and country clubs. Then we arranged to have our meetings streamed online – because we were a tribe, with a power that could transcend in-person energy. Now, each time someone else came onto any of our teams, they became instant tribe members, wherever they lived.

 Be Proactive in Your Company's Community.

Reach up and reach out. Surround yourself with the most helpful, positive people you can find. Give of yourself, and ask for what you need from others. If you don't see what you want, create it.

LA Connect helped significantly grow my team, my income, and my impact. But I was still having challenges; for instance, my terror of public speaking. I was working on it, but was I over it –

hah! Still fretting, still sweating, still forgetting. In fact, it was around this time that I famously passed out while presenting in front of eight people... in my own living room! #notagoodlook

I took that as a sign to either give up or get over it once and for all. I chose the latter. I joined a networking group where I was required to speak for... drumroll... 60 seconds a week. And I forced myself to speak at even more of our many team events.

I took baby steps, and babies fall. A lot. Yet eventually they walk. I may not have been ready for a TED Talk, but at least I never fainted again. And whatever I did was somehow good enough.

Hang Up Your Hang Ups.

They certainly don't serve you, and they only get in the way of your serving others.

I was getting good at having people join my team. However, I was unprepared for people quitting. Really, it shouldn't have been a surprise – most people quit on most things. But still.

The first person to quit was actually one of the first people to sign onto my team. Annie, let's call her, was a self-lit singer/songwriter and vocal coach who had said YES right away. She was smart, fearless, comfortable with sales, completely clear on her self-worth, and had been looking for a way to financially fuel herself despite her unpredictable passion career. Total Dream Teamer.

Then, one day, she called to say she was leaving. She'd gotten engaged. And her new fiancé was a guy with… let's just say, beaucoup de bucks. Her WHY had disappeared overnight.

I was crushed. Like, hit by a bus crushed.

But eventually I got over it. How? By realizing that this was part of the deal. By reminding myself that this business, like life itself, has no guarantees. And by understanding that it wasn't about me. When someone quits, they're not quitting on you. They're quitting on themselves.

 Don't Quit Just Because They Do.

Not everyone is meant to stay. People are on their own journeys. Trust that whatever happens will be for the best in the end.

And while some people quit, more were joining. More and more, actually. Actors, dancers, writers, cosmetologists, chefs, museum educators, teachers, lawyers – the range of people blew my mind. The momentum was palpable.

That year, I signed up for our Global Training Conference in Las Vegas. Larger Network Marketing companies typically have big annual meetings, and ours was legendary. But glitz, gambling, and crowds hold no magic for me. I went reluctantly, only because "plugging in" was part of the Blueprint. Luckily, some of my teamies were more excited to attend.

And yes, people partied like their lives depended on it. Yes, the casino and hotel were huge, loud, and a bit disorienting for extroverted introverts like me. HOWEVER... inside the MGM Grand Arena, I got a dose of the jaw-dropping electricity of our larger community. I witnessed the power of 18,000 people united to learn and grow, from top leaders inside the company and guest speaker gurus alike. It was like LA Connect on steroids.

Seeing dozens of teams, some of hundreds and even thousands, and watching so many achievers at all levels be recognized, was undeniable proof that the Blueprint worked. My team and I came back unstoppable.

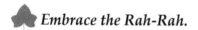 *Embrace the Rah-Rah.*

If it's your thing, WOO-HOO! If it's not, allow yourself to get swept up in the wave anyway, and see where it takes you.

We threw ourselves into our work, and I quickly elevated to the third of my company's four levels of success, called Regional Vice President, or RVP. Here, in addition to average monthly commissions and overrides of $4,000-10,000, you can earn a Mercedes Achiever Award of $800 a month to cover payment on a white Mercedes of your choice. I'd never been much of a car person, but I loved having a visible symbol of the success of our team's "invisible" online businesses.

Once again, I got there in average time – two years. However, this time, average felt pretty good. Claire and I had envisioned that we'd have our Mercedes "Car Party" together, and we did. It was at the Luxe Hotel in LA, with our teams, our friends, and our families, and it was a blast.

 Truly Celebrate Your Successes.

Never miss the chance to enjoy what you've earned – or to share the sweetness with those who've helped.

Yet the fun of "getting the keys" was no match for how it felt to GIVE the keys.

The first RVP keys went to my fantastic teamie Kim Starzyk. Handing them to her, I realized that this was a big part of what Network Marketing was REALLY about. In my law and music careers, I never had the opportunity to pay anything forward. I could get somewhere myself, but that didn't help anyone else get there. Here, I could help shift the entire course of someone's life for the better.

Kim had told me that jobs in her first love, acting, had largely stopped flowing when she hit her 40s (welcome to Hollywood). Real estate, her second career, paid well (or, more correctly, paid well WHEN it paid), but it wasn't emotionally satisfying. And even though she imagined it would be part time, it felt more full-time – and at the wrong times, like weekends. Not what she wanted as a mom.

By mentoring Kim to the RVP level, I helped her blossom from a frustrated freelancer into an empowered business owner. I watched her get to spend more time with her boys, let go of work that didn't move her, and take non-paying acting gigs just because she wanted to (Kim, if you're reading this, you rocked in *The Vagina Monologues*). The pleasure was profound.

Similar satisfaction came from supporting my next RVPs, Brook Dougherty and Deborah Hurwitz, to their goals. Brook's former careers ranged from advertising copywriter to VP of Sales and Marketing for an international film group. When we met, she was a philanthropist, running a foundation that focused on helping young people in the arts. She was excited to be able to contribute more to her cause through her Network Marketing earnings. And I was excited for her.

Deborah was a fellow literal Ivy leaguer – a Princeton grad – as well as a composer, conductor, and recording artist. Her bio was an accordion of accomplishments, from Sesame Street to Cirque du Soleil to the Broadway hit *Jersey Boys*. However, she'd taken a long-term position that had since lost its luster for her, and she yearned for freedom to focus on only what really moved her creatively. She built her Network Marketing business to create the additional revenue to regain that freedom. I could relate to that 100%, and so was 100% thrilled when she succeeded.

Of course, because of the way Network Marketing is structured, the success of each new leader on the team added to my own – without taking anything away from theirs.

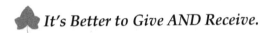 ## It's Better to Give AND Receive.

Lots had changed for the better for me. But one thing that remained stubbornly the same was my health – or rather, health challenge. Four years into my business, I was still struggling. Doctors finally identified an autoimmune disease called Hashimoto's. It's a thyroid issue, and exhaustion, cog fog, anxiety, and some other pesky problems, like constantly cold hands and feet, are all symptoms.

I did some research and learned that, like any autoimmune disease, Hashimoto's is incurable. I also learned that I wasn't alone – actually 14 million other Americans have it, and altogether between 24 and 50 million Americans have one or more autoimmune diseases. I suddenly had a lot more empathy for a lot more people. And I knew this was a test. Was I going to use my circumstances as an exit or an engine?

I chose the latter.

As I began employing everything from medication to meditation to improve my symptoms, I vowed that no matter how much time I spent in bed, or how achy, flaky, or shaky I sometimes felt, I was not going to let this condition stop me. In fact I suddenly felt a calling to step up and offer my solutions to a much larger population.

On the consumer side, I vowed to tell *everyone I knew* that they had an option for healthy products. On the business side, in addition to helping anyone looking for an escape plan from corporate or for a balm for the freelancer financial follies, I was determined to be a role model for anyone suffering with an autoimmune disease who needed a flexible way to earn additional revenue.

 ## Use Your Challenges as Fuel.

By year five, my business and my teammates' businesses had expanded even further. That growth lifted me to the top level of the company, which we call National Vice President or NVP. The average time to achieve this level is five years, so again, I was average. But this time I was delighted. Not only because at this level the average monthly earnings are over $20,000 per month (yes, you read that right), but because I'd done what I'd personally set out to do.

I'd created truly significant recurring revenue; in my case, building an asset that's now worth seven figures. And I'd hit this milestone while still writing songs, just as I'd desired. In fact, the same month I went NVP, I opened my first Broadway show as a lyricist – 12-hour rehearsal days and all.

It was pretty surreal. But I had a vision, a mission, and a TEAM. And we did it!

Claire and I had another party, because she too had become a National Vice President. We'd supported each other to the top, just as we'd vowed when we first met. It felt like half of LA Connect showed up to dance with us.

 Let Reality Meet Your Expectations.

Coincidentally, if you believe in coincidence, just before my diagnosis, my company had begun to offer a 30-day program focused on healthy living. It's a whole body reboot that helps people improve sleep, support a balanced gut, maintain a healthy weight, learn what foods do and don't serve their bodies, and develop better habits of self-care. After my diagnosis, I did the program. Now, I'm not making any medical claims about our products – that would be illegal. However, what I *can* say is that doing the program increased my energy and ability to focus BIG TIME. And that was exactly what I needed.

The program led me to feel clearer and more energized, and led me directly to my next VP, film producer Margaret French Isaac. After my success with the program, I began coaching others through it, including (after a particularly indulgent holiday season) my husband. When he posted, "Who wants to do this with me?" Margaret was the ONE person of his nearly 5,000 Facebook friends who responded, "ME!" And she committed to following the program 100%, despite her demanding job as Executive Vice President of Film and TV at Johnny Depp's production company, and being a busy mom of two teens.

Two weeks in, she was letting her whole world know that she felt like she'd gotten her mojo back. People were asking her what she was doing and how they could do it. She offered to refer them to me as clients, and I said, "Maybe you'd like to join me as a business partner, and have them as your clients instead." That's exactly what she did, climbing to the top 2% of earners in just 8 months. Her speed isn't typical, but neither is she!

 Trust That What Works for You Can Work for Others.

These last five years in my Network Marketing business have brought me more than I ever expected, not only financially, but in terms of the richness of the relationships I've been privileged to enjoy. I've been supported and fueled by hundreds of open, insightful people I otherwise would never have met. Some of them are teammates or sidelines, others are clients, some just folks I prospected, who simply turned out to be great friends.

Plus, I can't complain about earning a Caribbean cruise, a free suite for our Las Vegas meetings, beautiful resort vacations, that annual Maui trip, or being gifted bouquets on my birthday, roses on Valentine's Day, a wreath at Thanksgiving, a drawerful of Tiffany's jewelry, and dozens of other treats.

And as for the self-growth, well, what can I say? Sometimes I can hardly recognize myself. I feel exponentially more relaxed, and more confident. One year, in a plot twist I would never have imagined, I was asked to speak at our Global Training Conference. I knew this was a sign that I was finally ready to release my *"eyes on me"* trauma, and for the first time I was more excited than scared. During the talk, I was 100% present and calm. Afterwards, my feet literally felt like they weren't touching the ground. Now, I actually enjoy sharing my knowledge in front of larger groups.

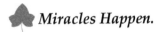 *Miracles Happen.*

If I sound like an evangelist, I feel like one. Is this nice Jewish girl a preacher? Or just a teacher? Call me whatever you want – I'm authentically sold on the benefits of what Network Marketing has to offer. I'm going to continue to keep choosing to create more for myself by helping more people create more for themselves. Hallelujah. Amen.

Chapter 11

More Ivy League Tips to the Top

Thus far, I've given you over three dozen Ivy League tips to help you become a successful professional Network Marketer. However, since Ivy Leaguers always go above and beyond, here are a few dozen more. They fit into four major categories. Embrace them, and you will see a seismic shift in your business, and, oh yeah, in your entire life.

 1. Treat Your Business Like a Business.

Ever hear that old adage that hobbies cost money and businesses make money? Well, it's still true. This is NetWORK Marketing, not NetPLAY Marketing. So:

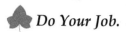 *Do Your Job.*

Network Marketing is not a job, but you need to do your job. That means do your own *Income Producing Activity* – inviting, sharing, following up, signing people up, helping with orders if need be – the things that can directly affect your bottom line – for at least an hour a day. Broken up into little bits is ok. More is better; less, not so much. And as we say, you can do this part-time, but you can't do it "sometimes."

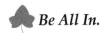 *Be All In.*

This business is designed to be part-time but not part-heart. So make every second you spend on your business about being *all in, in that moment.* You will get out of this what you put into it, so don't spend the time you put aside for your business analyzing or agonizing. A good way to be all in is to shut the back door. The one in your mind, that is. And hurl away the key.

An extra reward for following this tip is that it will help you be more present with whatever you're doing when you're NOT working, too. As it's said, the way you do anything is the way you do everything. So be all in here and you'll start to see positive crossover elsewhere.

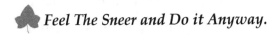 *Feel The Sneer and Do it Anyway.*

Doubters gonna doubt, haters gonna hate, behind your back and to your face.

And so what? When faced with disapproval, bush leaguers cave and Ivy Leaguers persist.

Anyone who's been in this business knows the drill. No matter who you are, or the way you do what you do, there are always those who don't or won't understand. My mentor Sue Cassidy – a charter member of the "what you think of me is none of my business" club – had a great, two question litmus test for sneerers. She'd ask, "Is this person paying your mortgage?" And

"Would they pay your hospital bills?" The answers are almost always no and no. So really, why are you letting *their* judgment determine *your* future?

When you are sure of the value of what you are doing, the fact that someone else doesn't value it is of no importance to you at all.

Get ready for people to think you're nuts. You will find resistance, very often among the people closest to you. As it's said, a prophet is not known in his own home. (And you know what? Neither, often, is a profit.)

Understand that some people won't understand. That's about them, and it's ok. Remember, we're not in the convincing business, we're in the sorting business. Sorting through which people we want to work with, have as clients, or listen to. Sorting through who's worth helping. Sorting through who's worth our time, our attention and our gifts.

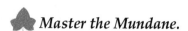 *Master the Mundane.*

Just like in any business, there will be some things in your Network Marketing business that will become (yawn) routine. That you will not feel are glam or cool. Like inviting another five people to hear about what you have to offer. Like offering people the same things over and over. Whenever you feel yourself going numb about the number of people you need to reach out to in order to have the results you want, relax. Remind yourself of your

WHY, imagine what it will feel like when you're already where you want to be, and find your curiosity in the next ask. If you want the magnificent, you have to deal with the monotonous. Expect the expected.

 To Get the Income, Detach From the Outcome.

You need to have passion for the action, a vision for where you are headed, and a bedrock of belief that you ARE achieving your goals. However, you also need to be detached from what happens in any one encounter. It's like dating. Becoming too stuck on whether "they're the ONE" puts you in a disempowered position. Getting too wrapped up in *how* everything will work out, or even in *who* it will happen with, will inevitably slow you down.

 Take a Vow to Allow.

Allowing is an action. This may feel counterintuitive, especially for those of us type As who were trained to do, do, do, because we mistakenly think that "more is always the cure." But ten actions – not preceded by one small intentional sail-setting breath – often yield nothing, while one short act of opening yourself up to allow success can bring about so-called "miraculous" change. As long as you are taking consistent action in your business, allowing in the positive results of that action, which you so rightly deserve, could be the most important action you take.

 ### Do What You Say You'll Do.

If you're SAYING you're reaching out to five new people a day, but what you're doing is going down the Instagram rabbit hole finding five new, fascinating people who you then DON'T reach out to, *stop*. And go do what you said you'd do.

Please don't ever utter the deadly words, "I'll try." "Trying" is a linguistic escape hatch to help you bail on yourself. And if you're overcome with terror and literally can't do one flippin' thing, listen to or read Mel Robbins' excellent book *The 5 Second Rule*. Then go do one flippin' thing.

 ### Don't Be Afraid of Ghosts.

Everyone gets ghosted. Sometimes it's personal, sometimes it's not. Learn not to care so much. And remember that Network Marketing is a realm where sometimes ghosts can come back to life. Especially if you add a little levity. One of my colleagues sends this to prospects who've gone MIA. It will often get a response and open the door to further discussion. "Hey, haven't heard back from you. Just wondering if a) you're super busy and just haven't had time to get back to me; b) I've done something to horribly offend you – if that's the case I'm so sorry, and I would love to know what I did, so I can learn from it; or c) you've been kidnapped by aliens and you really need my help."

And even when you don't hear back in the moment, it doesn't necessarily mean you will never hear. Sometimes people are watching you, and when you succeed, they'll "rise from the dead."

 ### *Remember That It's a Numbers Game.*

Whether you're thinking about prospects, clients, or teammates, the truth is always the same. You can't control them, you can't command them, and you'll never keep 100% of them. Not even close. Luckily, you don't need 100%, or anywhere near it, to have a viable business. What you DO need is a steady stream of people to whom you can OFFER what you have. A significant number of people every month. On my team, I say, "Forty faces gets you places," meaning getting our business and our products in front of forty people a month is enough, in general, to have a real business.

 ### *Take Your Time.*

In any business, success doesn't come overnight, so stop expecting it to. Patience is a gift only you can give yourself. If you're feeling impatient, put down the stopwatch and give yourself some time to get the hang of this. Some time to learn what you're doing. Some time to start showing a profit.

Give Yourself a Quarterly Review.

Pretend you're the boss. Actually, you don't even have to pretend – you <u>are</u> the boss. With the work that you are doing now, the way you are doing it, and the attitude you're doing it with, would you hire you? Keep you on? Give you a raise or a bonus? Bosses expect people to show up. They expect people to be good for their word. They expect people to do their best, not just phone it in. They expect people to leave their personal dramas at the door, and be productive.

 Don't Quit Before Payday.

Most people start their Network Marketing businesses and then quit the first (or second or fifth) time something doesn't work out. Ivy League it and don't be most people.

And remember, "don't quit before payday" is way different from just "don't quit." "Don't quit" is your first step towards success, but not your last. Don't quit before you get where you said you wanted to go. Don't quit before your checks – and the life and impact they afford you – match your dreams. Don't quit before your mission is accomplished. Just follow your leaders. Unless *they* quit. Then follow THEIR leaders – the smart ones who are still here.

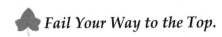 *Fail Your Way to the Top.*

Everyone makes mistakes. So why do we pretend we're not everyone? When you learn from your mistakes, you'll earn from your mistakes. Failure is an essential part of the process. Expect it and embrace it as a guide. Keep what works, change what doesn't. There is no fail. Just succeed or learn. Or, in this case, learn to succeed.

2. Train Your Brain.

Success starts and ends between your ears. So here are some things to remember:

 Keep Your WHY Top of Mind.

Why are you doing this business? No, really... why? You need to know it like you know your name. Because between our vices and our devices, distraction can be our default mode, unless there's a compelling reason otherwise. Your WHY is that reason. And just because you came face-to-face with yourself, got real, and wrote it down *once* doesn't mean you're thinking about it regularly. In fact, many big issues are easier to push to the back of our emotional closets. You need to get in there and pull them forward. Remember why you're doing this. Remind yourself for what and for whom you're doing this. If it's important to you, you'll find a way. If it's not, you'll find an excuse.

Shift the Thoughts That are Running You.

Conscious thoughts are always only the tip of the psychological iceberg, and what's under that water is *chilly*. Whether you're reacting to current dream stealers, naysayers, family, friends, or to negative programming drummed into you long ago, if you are a human, you'll have some unhelpful thoughts (ok, maybe tens of thousands a day) that will hurt your business if you don't deal with them. Get under the surface and get to work melting your inner cray-cray.

Thought-shifting is totally personal, so what resonates with you could be affirmations, prayer, meditation, medication... whatever it takes to be in control of your unconscious thoughts, instead of the other way around.

You might want to read or watch marvellously wise coach Marcia Wieder *(Dream, Doing Less and Having More)*, or T. Harv Eker *(Secrets of the Millionaire Mind)*.

Or perhaps try Tapping (aka: EFT, or Emotional Freedom Technique). Tapping is a well-known, simple method of literally tapping on specific energy meridian points on your body while attuning to thoughts that you speak out aloud. Through tapping, you can turn down the emotional volume of negative thoughts and ramp up positive thoughts. Tapping puts change literally at your fingertips, allowing you, over time, to transform what you think and how those thoughts feel. Margaret Lynch Raniere *(Tapping Into Wealth)* is one of my faves in this area.

Or, Run Your Energy. This is a powerful method of magnetizing more of what you want that was created by my fabulous friend and personal Manifestation Coach (yes, they exist), Heidi Baker. Here, you narrate, out loud, the *exact* future you want as *if it actually just happened*, and describe it in vivid detail, with as much excitement as if you are speaking to your best friend. Don't knock it 'til you've tried it – it's addictive. Putting the future into the present tense, heating up the excitement, and remaining in this state for even just 5-10 minutes can create palpable shifts in your day.

You'll know when something is working. For myself, I actually have created a hybrid where I run my energy WHILE tapping. Turbocharged!

 *Underthink It.*

In Network Marketing, you don't get any points for knowing the most. This is an "**act**-ivity" based business, not a "**think**-tivity' based business. Instinct, action, and course correction are a much better trio than research, restraint, and resistance. Overthinking is the sign of a perfectionistic mind. It leads to underacting, which leads to underearning.

When you catch yourself overthinking, **pivot.** Forgive yourself immediately, and take the next income-producing *action*, right away.

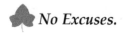 *No Excuses.*

Excuses stink like farts in an elevator. If you catch yourself making one – *especially to yourself* – admit it. Wave your hand to clear the air. Say, pardon me. Because you can have excuses or you can have results, but you can't have both. If you are looking for a reason to leave, plateau, or lose, you will always find it. But if you are looking for a reason to stay, rise, and thrive, you will find that too.

What some people would use as excuses, others seize as motivation to plow ahead. Reema Rafay, an NVP in our company and a Canadian-born Muslim, faced decades of bullying for her heritage, at times being physically abused and even being told "you're better off dead. " She could have bought into others' beliefs that she was worthless, but decided instead to triumph – to show herself and others that nothing was out of reach. She built her Network Marketing business while running her own Executive Search company and being an actively involved mom and wife. How? "I won't feed into excuses. Period."

 3. Regulate Your Emotional Temperature.

Just like you need to mind your mind, you need to control the thermostat on your feelings.

Your Comfort Zone is Your Danger Zone.

You can't stay small and have big results. Small people with small minds and small dreams have small impact, small influence, and small success.

To play a bigger game, growth is required, not optional. If you're feeling comfortable, it's a sign you're not playing a big enough game.

Be willing to get comfortable with being uncomfortable. Grow your belief. Grow your skills. Grow your vision. And grow a pair, if you haven't already.

 ## *If You Compare, You Will Despair.*

This is the phrase I used when my kids were young and used to fight over whose Rocky Road ice cream scoop was bigger (sigh). But nothing changes when you're older. You don't win by comparing your portion, or your journey, to anyone else's. Life makes this lesson available to us daily. Unless you are looking at where someone else is, or how fast they got there, *purely for inspiration* for what you can do, just stop looking. Be yourself every time. That in itself is a win.

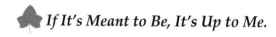

If It's Meant to Be, It's Up to Me.

Use this as your mantra. Yes, you are building a team, and "teamwork makes the dream work." But in the end, it's on you. The buck stops here or the bucks stop here. YOU are the engine of your own business. Your commitment to YOUR part – doing YOUR activity, raising YOUR game, clearing any blocks of YOURS – is what matters most. Your business can only be as big as you are.

It's Not About You.

But wait, didn't you just say, "if it's meant to be, it's up to me?" YES, but that doesn't mean to make it all about you.

Of course, you started this for you. You want what you want. But that's not in the slightest bit relevant to anyone but you... and maybe your mom.

Remind yourself that you only get what you want by helping others get what they want, both on the business side and on the product side of your biz. So, look to serve people and trust that the results will come. You want what you want for you, but really what most other people care about is WHAT'S IN IT FOR THEM. And unless and until THEY feel you have THEIR best interests at heart, YOU will not succeed to your highest potential.

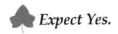 **Expect Yes.**

I have heard many people in Network Marketing say that you should "go for no," which is really their way of saying, "You're going to have to ask a *lot* of people to take a look at what you're offering before you get enough yesses, so get busy asking a lot of people, and don't be put off by the "no's" along the way."

However, as a mindset, **go for no** always shut me down. *Expect yes* worked much better. Why jump into action with anything less than an attitude that of course, people will **say yes**?

Not that you need to break down in shock when people just plain old don't want what you're offering. Get a grip. Expecting yes doesn't mean you'll always get it. But to me, it's much more powerful than starting from the negative.

Best case, you get what you expect. Middle case, you get a no for now, and the possibility of a yes later. Worst case, you get a big fat NOTHING. Which is why you need to…

 **Learn How to Lose.**

I got this phrase from my then 18-year-old teammate, Zoë Almanza, who got recruited to play volleyball at the University of Oregon. She said, "First rule of any sport, **you will not always win… so be prepared.** It's built into what sports is all about." Network Marketing is like that. You practice, you envision success, you play full out, and when you win, you are not surprised. But when you lose, you are not crushed.

If at first you don't succeed, cry for five minutes. Not every time, please. Oh, and you don't get any boo-hoo time if you've been half-assing your work. But if you are really, really doing the do and something goes sideways, you are allowed to turn on the waterworks if you want to. In fact, it's much better than burying hurt and resentment. Just remember to be in a private space when you do it. Let out the ***tension!*** Then remember your ***intention*** and refocus your ***attention*** on the things that serve you and the people you are here to assist.

Bouncing back is a skill. It needs to be learned and practiced. Your bounce back speed – from a no, a conversation gone sideways, a bad month, ANY setback – will determine the ultimate health of your business. So, intend to bounce back a little faster. And then a little faster, until finally, you ***have a rubber butt.*** Get knocked down, bounce back up right away.

 Don't Let Doubt Take You Out.

This little rhyme, created by a famous coach to consultants in my company, Jerry Roisentul, contains big wisdom. Doubt is not the issue. The issue is how you deal with it. You can have doubt, address it, work through it, and allow yourself to rise, or you can have doubt, ignore it, let it get the better of you, and take your business down, down, down. Everyone has doubt at some time, about something. Learn to let it go.

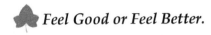 *Feel Good or Feel Better.*

This is the essence of the book *Ask and It Is Given*, the Esther and Jerry Hicks classic, helpfully restated for more modern audiences in Gabrielle Bernstein's *Super Attractor*. Feeling good more often is the central emotional driver of success. Focus on it, allow it, command it, expand it. And whenever you can't feel good, feel better. Just a little bit. You will definitely need to use your imagination sometimes, and in the beginning, maybe most of the time. Get brave and trick yourself, just for a minute at a time, into expanding your imagination so that you FEEL GOOD, or at least decent, doing, experiencing, and receiving more and more.

 4. Be A Pro, Not A Schmo.

Manners count, so please use them. No shoving things down people's throats. That kind of crap is what gives Network Marketers a bad rap. To Ivy up:

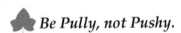 *Be Pully, not Pushy.*

Resist the urge to vomit about your fantastic company and products. A little goes a long way. So say a *little* something. Then... pause. Ask a question. Be on the lookout for indicators of need or desire for what you have to offer. Talk a little, then listen a lot. As they say, that's why we have two ears and one mouth.

 ### *Model Good Moral Hygiene.*

Treat people the way you'd like to be treated. No one owes you anything. If they're kind enough to be open to what you are offering, be grateful and gracious. And whatever happens, remember that not every business, or product, is right for everyone. That's fine. More than fine.

 ### *Remain Human.*

Whether you're doing your biz in person or on social media, don't morph into a sales-bot the minute you start your Network Marketing business. Don't get all weird and just chat or post endlessly about your company and their products. That only makes other people suspicious that you've joined a cult, and gives the rest of us Network Marketing normies unnecessary work undoing our prospects' prejudices.

Use the WAIT Method.

WAIT = Why Am I Talking? If you don't know, shut up and listen. Use this method in every interaction. Are you over-talking because you're looking to show your superior knowledge? People don't care. Or because you're afraid of hearing no? People don't care. It's in the silence that prospects feel free to say what's really on their minds.

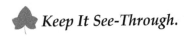 *Keep It See-Through.*

Transparency is key in Network Marketing as well as life in general. Be upfront. Say you're reaching out for a business reason. Say you just started your business and you don't have all the answers – that's why you'd like to loop in your mentor. Say you'd love to have someone on your team – IF you actually would. Say you *sucked-so-bad* and want a do-over. Whatever.

 5. Practice Healthy Habits.

Your Network Marketing biz is no different than anything else in life – small steps in the right direction, taken regularly, produce big results. Therefore...

 Start Your Day Right.

Just like you need breakfast for your body, you need "breakfast for your business."

Hal Elrod's *The Miracle Morning* gives a simple way to "habit stack" six positive habits for a tasty mental meal. His calls them S.A.V.E.R.S.: Silence (purposeful silence, e.g. reflection, prayer, deep breathing); Affirmations (positive statements of who you are being and what you're doing); Visualization (your ideal day, how things go your way, where this is leading you); Exercise (any kind, no biggie); Reading (inspirational or informational books or trainings); and Scribing (writing out what you're grateful for, what you're learning, breakthroughs, realizations, and what you're committed to creating). This process can take 60 minutes if you have it, as little as six if you don't.

 Be a Slave to Your Calendar.

My calendar is my bitch. If it's in it, I do it. If it's not, it likely doesn't happen. Book the times you will definitely be working your business, and keep your appointments, including (and especially) the ones with yourself.

 Embrace Work Rituals.

Throughout the day, use habits to your advantage. This might mean completing a daily activity sheet provided by your mentor or company, going to a specific space and place to work (yes, your car can count), utilizing online 'parallel play for parallel pay' times with colleagues… whatever you choose that yields consistent results.

One useful ritual is to "Eat that Frog." This idea is from Brian Tracy's book of the same title. It means figuring out what the most important yet likely most distasteful thing you need to do is every day, and doing it *first*. If there's an important reach out you are particularly afraid to make, do it first. If you're falling apart because you're freaked out about a follow-up, do it first. It can only get easier from there.

Another ritual I love is using an app called Centered, which blissfully combines productivity and serenity. Centered allows you to integrate calendars, organize your time, get the dopamine hit of successful task completion, utilize calming playlists, and experience quick, inspiring hacks for brain, body, and work.

 Say "I Get To" instead of "I Have To."

Obligation can feel like a drag. We have enough of that in other parts of our lives. Network Marketing is a choice, not an obligation. When you're feeling stressed or exhausted, flip the script. Remind yourself that you don't have to participate in this burgeoning business model, you **get** to. You **get to** do reach outs. You **get** to check things off your to do list. You **get to** keep your appointments. You **get to** uplevel your life. **You get to** create a world with more extra money, more choices, more community, and more impact than you have had before. Shifting this one phrase can instantly alter how you feel about what you're doing. And that can uplevel your entire business.

 Choose Gratitude, not Attitude.

That may sound like a (rhyme alert) platitude, and, ok, it is. But it only got so popular because it's TRUE. You can't feel grateful and depressed, angry, or stuck at the same time. So be grateful for this opportunity. Be grateful for the people who created this opportunity, and the ones who brought it to you. Be grateful to yourself for saying yes. Be grateful for every referral. Be grateful for every client. Be grateful to your team of business partners. And if you don't have a team yet, be grateful for the one that's coming.

Before you go, two important reminders. First:

 Don't Give Anyone a Crystal Ball for Your Life.

What you see for YOURSELF must remain paramount. Others love to enroll us in their visions for what's true and what's possible, even if they are limiting, fear-based, and false. Even when they are not seeing life through our eyes. While you are here on the planet, YOU have the power to dream and declare, to decide and to do, whatever is right for YOU. If you relinquish your power to anyone with a smaller desire or fire than you, you will leave this world unfulfilled.

And last, but not in the least bit least:

 Work It, 'Cuz It's Worth It.

Pinky swear.

Resource List

If you are joining us in this profession, here are some of the key books, authors, speakers and coaches who've impacted me personally, and whom I recommend.

<u>*Dare to Dream, Work to Win*</u> by Dr. Tom Barrett, Ph. D.

A foundational Network Marketing book. Ex-Network Marketing sceptic Tom Barrett's doctorate is in Psychology, so there's as much light shed on what's going on inside you, and the psychology of entrepreneurship, as there is on the value of Network Marketing from a business point of view. Use this to, as he says, "understand the dollars and sense of success in Network Marketing," further your understanding of both the business and yourself, shift your negative self talk, and boost your leadership skills. See <u>www.daretodream.net</u>.

<u>*Go Pro*</u> by Eric Worre

Go Pro is an industry classic: a 7 step, to the point, power packed overview on how and why to do Network Marketing right. Now, Eric Worre has a YouTube Channel, and co-hosts top level events. I highly recommend you follow him and soak up as much of what he and the people he interviews have to offer as you can. He is continually offering information to help any Network Marketing professional up their game. See <u>www.networkmarketingpro.com</u>.

<u>*The Four Year Career*</u> and <u>*Mach 2*</u> by Richard Bliss Brooke

More industry classic quick reads. *The Four Year Career* reminds the reader right on the cover that their life is up to them, declaring the book shows "how to make your dreams of fun and financial freedom come true... *or not!*" As well as talking through the basics, Brooke dives deep into the potential asset value of working a Network Marketing business. *Mach 2* elucidates how and why to build a strong vision for success and have it take root in your subconscious. At 22, Brooke left a job at a chicken processing plant and built a multi-million dollar network marketing business. He now runs a top level coaching business for Network Marketing professionals. Check out his podcast The Authentic Networker and www.richardbrooke.com.

<u>*Get Over Your Damn Self*</u> by Romi Neustadt

Fellow recovering lawyer and former PR Exec Romi tells it like it is. The Network Marketing company she reps sells mostly women's products, so her language is female-centric and largely mom-oriented, but there are gems a-plenty for all genders. I especially like her chapter "F Fear", which lists 100 common fears to neutralize. See www.romineustadt.com.

<u>*Rich Dad, Poor Dad*</u> by Robert Kiyosaki

This book, subtitled "What The Rich Teach Their Kids About Money That the Poor and Middle Class Do Not!", is the #1 best selling personal finance book of all time, and for good reason. It tells the story of Kiyosaki's "safe job" real father ("Poor Dad"), the entrepreneurial father of his best friend ("Rich Dad") – and the ways in which both men shaped his thoughts about money and investing. Clearly, he's a fan of the "Rich Dad's" financial attitude and aptitude, and he generously walks you through ways you can to begin to make "Rich Dad" choices. Kiyosaki considers Network Marketing a "Rich Dad" option. See www.richdad.com.

Secrets of the Millionaire Mind by T. Harv Eker

If you're experiencing 'earnorexia' – feeling habitually stuck at a lower than desired income level – or you're in the habit of earning a lot and having it disappear just as quickly, this New York Times #1 bestselling book could change it all – assuming you commit to taking the time and actually doing the actions suggested. In a casual yet compelling style, Eker helps you "master the inner game of wealth" by discovering your current "money blueprint", embracing fundamental wealth principles, losing the limiting beliefs, and reprogramming yourself to have a "millionaire mindset." See www.harvekeronline.com.

Tapping Into Wealth by Margaret Lynch Raniere

Another great angle on the money issue. Self-worth is connected to net worth, and Lynch – a trained chemical engineer and ex-Fortune 500 sales and management exec – shows you how to elevate both, using tapping, a deeply effective mind-body tool. It can help you deprogram old money beliefs, "shatter your inner glass ceiling," and allow goal setting and goal getting to be motivating, not stressful. Who wouldn't want to "tap into" that? See www.margaretlynchraniere.com.

The Miracle Morning by Hal Elrod

Subtitled "The Not-So-Obvious Secret Guaranteed To Transform Your Life (Before 8 AM)", this book promises a LOT. And it delivers – again, if you do. Elrod's international bestseller helps you set your sail in the right direction every single day in six simple steps. It centers around the truth that successful people approach mornings as a critical time to influence their attitudes and impact their actions for the rest of the day; and walks you through how to focus on yourself and your intentions each morning to live in alignment with your long term goals. See www.halelrod.com.

The Slight Edge by Jeff Olson

This short, insightful book demonstrates the profoundly positive effects of small positive choices, chosen repeatedly. It explains the importance of getting the little things right, and the big consequences of getting them wrong. It can motivate you to stop "starting and stopping" what's truly beneficial, and to develop the simple daily discipline of choosing to DO the things that are "easy to do, easy not to do". Olson was the founder of a major Network Marketing company, and his wisdom is this business model. See www.amazon.com/Jeff-Olson.

The 5 Second Rule: Transform your Life, Work and Confidence with Everyday Courage by Mel Robbins

Fellow attorney Robbins rose from the depths of despair to the peak of personal empowerment when she figured out a guaranteed 5 second work-around to procrastination, fear and self-sabotage. As she discovered, "Five seconds is how fast your self-doubt kicks in and your mind goes to work against you. That's why you have to move even faster." If a 5 second solution sounds too simple to be true, it's not. Now Robbins is the most booked female speaker in the world, with good reason. Catch her super popular TEDx talk or see www.melrobbins.com.

The Wealthy Spirit: Daily Affirmations for Financial Stress Reduction by Chellie Campbell

Financial Stress Reduction ® speaker, author and coach Campbell is as real as they come. An actor turned bookkeeping business owner turned inspired educator, she playfully engages you to ditch your crazies and up your game, to practical effect. As Mark Victor Hansen, co-author of the uber popular *Chicken Soup for the Soul* series, says: "Read a page a day to multiply your money, decrease your stress and vastly improve your life and lifestyle!" Chelie's other books, *From Worry to Wealthy: A Woman's Guide to Financial Success Without the Stress* and *Zero to Zillionaire*, are equally fun, honest, pithy and chock full of great ideas. See www.chellie.com.

Dream: Clarify and Create What You Want by Marcia Wieder

Visionary thinker, humanitarian, coach, *Oprah* show regular and best-selling author Wieder wrote *Dream* to help you identify the things that matter to you most, then create and design a life that fully expresses your purpose. And since she also taught at Stanford Business School, was the president of the National Association of Women Business Owners, and assisted 3 U.S. Presidents, it's as much about doing as dreaming. Marcia is the CEO/Founder Dream University ® and member of the Transformational Leadership Council (TLC), composed of leaders in the transformational consciousness space such as Jack Canfield, Stephen Covey, and others. See www.marciawieder.com.

Super Attractor by Gabrielle Bernstein

This book, by New York Times #1 best seller, speaker and self-transformation guru Gabrielle Bernstein, invites you through the spiritual door to success. She provides specific methods to tap into abundance and joy, take spiritually aligned action, release the binds of the past, and create a better future, one good-feeling thought at a time. This is not necessarily a business book, however, if you're even the slightest bit woo woo, this could be a total game-changer in learning how to attract what you want – in your business, and everywhere else, too. See www.gabbybernstein.com.

Coach Jerry Roisentul: Jerry had a successful career with a major Network Marketing company prior to becoming a certified Coach, Speaker and Trainer with the John Maxwell Group. He speaks from deep experience and has a true heart to help people rise. Listening to him, you can instantly feel that nothing is more important to him than your success. Jerry's passion is sharing leadership principles with corporations and individuals inside and outside of Network Marketing. He has a devoted following inside my company and elsewhere. See www.championmentorship.com.

Coach Heidi Baker: Heidi is a master Manifestation Coach whose unique self-empowerment method, called "Running Your Energy," has helped clients worldwide attain what they truly desire. A former dental hygienist who turned her passion for home improvement into a $48 million business in under 4 years, she is a firm believer that when you change how you think and feel, anything and everything becomes possible. Heidi teaches audiences & clients alike how to get what they want out of work, life, finances and even romance. Working with her can help you let your long hidden genie out of its bottle! See www.expertredefined.com.

CPSIA information can be obtained
at www.ICGtesting.com
Printed in the USA
LVHW081500230321
682224LV00055BA/1545